Developing Reading Fluency

Grade 5

Written by
Trisha Callella

Editor: Alaska Hults
Illustrator: Ann Iosa
Designer/Production: Mary Gagné/Carmela Murray
Cover Designer: Mary Gagné
Art Director: Tom Cochrane
Project Director: Carolea Williams

Table of Contents

Introduction

Learning to read is a systematic, learned process. Once students can read individual words, they need to learn to put those words together to form sentences. Then, students must learn to read those sentences fluently to comprehend the meaning of each word and the meaning of an entire sentence. Students' reading fluency develops as they learn to break sentences into phrases and to "chunk" words together into phrases as they read. As students read sentences in phrases, they develop better comprehension of each sentence's meaning, read at a faster pace, and read with increased expression and intonation.

Use the lessons in *Developing Reading Fluency* to meet district, state, and national reading standards as you teach students how to develop reading fluency. The first section contains informal assessments you can use to help determine what skills students have mastered, what they are using poorly or inconsistently, and where the skill gaps are in their reading. The remaining sections are arranged sequentially to help you implement fluency modeling, fluency practice by students, and students' application of fluency strategies. Use the activities to help students build upon the skills they learned in the previous section. The final section of the book contains additional instruction to provide intervention for students having difficulties. The book features the following strategies to improve students' reading fluency:

- **Read-Arounds:** Help students learn high-frequency and content words and practice reading text in phrases as they work in small groups.
- **Phrasing Fun:** Guide students as they practice reading words in a sentence chunked by meaning. Then, have them apply this skill to a longer section of related text.
- **Phrased Text:** Have students read paragraphs where the chunked phrases are visually cued. Then, immediately have students reread the same text without the visual cues.
- **Reader's Theater:** Have students work in groups of four to practice rereading a script until they can fluently read their part in front of an audience. Use the performances as a culminating activity to have students apply all the reading strategies they have learned.
- **Intervention Activities:** Use these activities with individuals or small groups to intervene with students who still struggle with reading fluency. These activities enable students to identify and practice expression, intonation, and the natural flow of fluency.

The activities in this book provide students with a variety of reading experiences. The themes and genres included in each section will motivate students to not only read the text but to read with expression, intonation, and a natural flow. Students will build enthusiasm and confidence as they begin to increase their comprehension and as they successfully apply reading strategies to their everyday reading!

Reading fluency is the ability to read with expression, intonation, and a natural flow that sounds like talking. Fluency is not the speed at which one reads. That is the reading rate. A fluent reader does read quickly; however, he or she also focuses on phrased units of meaning. A student may read quickly but may not necessarily be fluent. Students who read too quickly often skip over punctuation. This inhibits comprehension because punctuation helps convey the meaning. Fluent readers have developed automaticity. This means that they have a solid bank of sight words on which they can rely and that are automatic. Fluent readers can then focus their reading on understanding the message rather than decoding the text. Reading is decoding with comprehension. Fluent readers do both. They read without thinking about how they are reading, and they understand what they are reading.

What does a student who lacks fluency sound like?

A student who lacks fluency may sound choppy, robotic, or speedy.

How does repeated oral reading increase fluency?

Research shows that students increase their fluency when they read and reread the same passage aloud several times. The support that teachers give students during oral reading by modeling the text and providing guidance and feedback enhances their fluency development. Using this strategy, students gradually become better readers and their word recognition, speed, accuracy, and fluency all increase as a result. Their comprehension also improves because they are bridging the gap between reading for word recognition and reading for meaning.

Why is it so critical for fifth graders to read with fluency?

Bad habits can be hard to break. By this time, the student has had six years to practice and transfer reading skills and strategies. Any student who is not reading with fluency in fifth grade is not comprehending the text. This is especially worrisome since the fifth grader must comprehend nonfiction text well in order to succeed in other content areas. Implement the activities and strategies included in this book to guide the learner to reading fluently.

How do fluency and phrasing work together?

Phrasing is the link between decoding the meaning of the text and reading the text fluently. Phrasing is how a reader groups words in a sentence. A lack of phrasing results in staccato reading, "word calling," and decoding. A fluent reader reads in phrased chunks that are meaningful. Read the information on page 5 to learn more about phrasing.

A student who reads in phrases reads words in meaningful groups. Phrasing helps a student understand that the text carries meaning. A phrase is a group of words that the reader says together and reads together. The way the words are grouped affects the meaning. This is why phrasing affects reading comprehension.

What does phrasing sound like?

Consider how the same sentence can have different meanings depending on the way the words are grouped, or phrased. It clearly affects the comprehension of what is read. For example:

> Patti Lee is my best friend.
>
> Patti, Lee is my best friend.

Who is the best friend? It depends on how the sentence is read. In this example, punctuation also affects phrasing.

What causes incorrect phrasing?

A student may read with incorrect phrasing for a number of reasons. First, many students rely too much on phonics. This leads to a dependency on decoding. When students focus on decoding, they neglect the message. They turn into expert "word callers." Incorrect phrasing can also result from a lack of attention to punctuation. Some students ignore punctuation altogether, which will result in incorrect phrasing, affect their fluency, and hurt their comprehension.

What can I do to teach and improve phrasing?

1. Use the activities in this book. They are all researched, teacher-tested, and student-approved, and they will help students experience reading fluency success.

2. Photocopy a story, a student's writing sample, or a poem onto an overhead transparency. As the class reads it together, mark off the phrases using a steady sweep of a transparency marker to visually show the voiced phrases. (The sweep should look like a flattened *u* that extends from the start to the end of the phrase.) This visual-auditory connection benefits those students who are still not reading fluently.

3. Read and reread.

4. Model. Model. Model.

5. Echo read.

6. Make flash cards of common phrases to help students train their eyes to see words in groups rather than as individual words.

7. Tape-record students as they read. Let them listen to improvements they make in phrasing and intonation.

8. Write multisyllabic words on index cards. Have students practice decoding them. Teach strategies of looking for known chunks in words and applying meaning to those chunks. As students become more efficient at breaking down multisyllabic words into meaningful chunks, they are able to focus on the meaning of the words, read more fluently, and comprehend more of what is read.

Getting Started

How to Use This Book

The activities in this book provide fun and easy strategies that will help students develop reading fluency. Getting started is simple.

- Read the Stages of Fluency Development chart on page 7. Then, use the assessments that begin on page 10 to determine students' needs. Read the directions carefully to understand the modifications to traditional informal reading inventories. Use this information to create a plan of action and decide on which skills the whole class, groups of students, and individuals need to focus.
- Use the Fantastic Five Format on page 8 with the whole class, small groups, or individuals. This format provides a guideline for developing reading fluency that will work with any genre. Copy the reproducible, and use it as a "cheat sheet" when you give guided instruction. You will find the format effective in helping you with modeling, teaching, guiding, and transferring phrased and fluent reading to independent reading.
- Refer to the Teacher Tips on page 9 before you begin using the activities in this book. These tips include helpful information that will assist you as you teach all students in your classroom to read fluently and, as a result, improve their comprehension of text.

Fluency Activities and Strategies

The sections of this book have been sequentially arranged for you to first model fluency, then have students practice fluency, and finally have them independently apply their newly learned skills. Each section has an introductory page to help you get started. It includes

- an explanation of how the activities in that section relate to fluency development
- the strategies students will use to complete the activities
- a materials list
- step-by-step directions for preparing and presenting the activities
- an idea for how to vary the activities

Each section opener is followed by a set of fun reproducible reading materials that are designed to excite and motivate students about developing reading fluency. Within each section, the readability of the reproducibles increases in difficulty to provide appropriate reading material for fifth graders who read at different levels.

Intervention Activities and Strategies

The Intervention Activities section is designed for students who are struggling with fluency. They need direct, systematic instruction in a one-on-one format where you can instruct at the point of difficulty. These five activities provide that opportunity. Some may also work well in a very small group. The activities are designed for intensive instruction to change bad habits and instill solid strategies for reading fluently.

Stages of Fluency Development

Stage	What You Observe	What to Teach for Fluency
1	• many miscues • too much emphasis on meaning • storytelling based on pictures • sounds fluent but not reading what is written down • playing "teacher" while reading	• print carries the meaning
2	• tries to match what he or she says with what is written on the page • one-to-one correspondence • finger pointing and "voice pointing" • staccato reading, robotic reading	• phrasing and fluency • focus on meaning • read like talking • high-frequency words • purpose of punctuation
3	• focuses on the meaning of print • may use bookmark • focuses more on print than picture • no longer voice points • laughs, giggles, or comments while reading	• phrasing and fluency • focus on what makes sense and looks right • purpose of punctuation • proper expression and intonation
4	• reads books with more print than pictures • wants to talk about what he or she read • reads like talking with phrasing • reads punctuation with expression • laughs, giggles, or comments while reading	• shades of meaning • making connections
5	• reads and comprehends novels and some nonfiction text • reads with 4- to 5-word phrases that match natural speech • reads punctuation with expression • changes voice for different characters or speakers when reading aloud • laughs, giggles, or comments while reading • reads in phrases both silently and orally	• multisyllabic word decoding for meaningful chunks • fluency in nonfiction text • shades of meaning • making connections • fluent reading with advanced punctuation—broken syllables at ends of lines, hyphens, parentheses
6	• reads and comprehends novels and nonfiction text • reads with 5 or more words in phrases that match natural speech • reads advanced punctuation with proper intonation (hyphens, parentheses, semicolons, split syllables at ends of lines, asides, etc.) • changes voice to match tone of the story (intonation sounds grim, excited, etc.) • changes voice to match characters, setting, surroundings, foreshadowing • laughs, giggles, or comments while reading • makes connections while reading (interacts with the text) • reads nonfiction text fluently	This is a fluent reader. Fluent readers just need further practice on material with increasing vocabulary demands.

Fantastic Five Format

Modeled Fluency

Model reading with fluency so that students understand the text and what they are supposed to learn.

Echo Reading

Read one part. Have students repeat the same part.

Choral Reading

Read together. This prepares students to take over the task of reading.

Independent Fluency

Have students read to you.

Reverse Echo Reading

Have students read to you, and then repeat their phrasing, expression, and fluency. Students have now taken over the task of reading.

Developing Reading Fluency • Gr. 5 © 2004 Creative Teaching Press

Teacher Tips

1. Teach students who are struggling with fluency and phrasing in guided reading groups. However, be flexible in your grouping. If you are teaching a fluency strategy, then you can group them together. If you are teaching a comprehension strategy or skill, they should be in a mixed guided reading group. This is especially important for fifth-grade students, since they probably have been grouped with the same struggling students since kindergarten. When this occurs, they do not have any daily models of fluent reading aside from you. They must interact with fluent readers in the class. The activities in this book provide many additional opportunities to make sure that these students work with everyone—not just other struggling readers.

2. When asking students to read aloud in class during science, social studies, or reading, give them time to browse the material first. This helps the struggling student get the whole picture before it is broken down.

3. When asking students to read aloud in class, choose names at random by using a flip-up index card booklet or sticks with the students' names on them. When students are chosen at random, everyone pays attention to all of the reading and the struggling students have a higher level of comprehension.

4. Another important thing to remember is that students naturally want to help one another. When a struggling reader reads aloud for the class, fluent readers commonly "help" by telling the student words or phrases to read. Struggling students are often given significantly less time to solve a reading problem than fluent readers are. Try to eliminate that helping. Instead say, "He (or she) can do it," and wait. When given a chance, students will achieve.

5. Do not invite students to use their finger to track while reading. It is a bad habit that trains the eyes to look at only one word at a time. If a student continuously loses his or her place, tell the student to put his or her finger at the beginning of that line of text and move from line to line.

6. If students use bookmarks, have them hold the bookmark just above the line of print they are reading rather than just under the line. When students use a bookmark under a line of print, the bookmark blocks the next line. This keeps students from reading fluently because they cannot see the ending punctuation to anticipate the intonation and expression needed.

7. Teach your students how you mark the phrases read when they read aloud to you. Have practice sessions where they work with random partners to listen and record phrases the partner reads.

Informal Reading Inventories

This section of the book is dedicated to ongoing individual assessment to determine what a student knows, what is used but confused, and what needs further development in the area of reading. The reading selections will give you the opportunity to monitor growth and guide your instruction based on individual needs. Each selection will tell you the following about the student:

1. ability to decode fifth-grade nonfiction reading material (goal: read to learn)

2. the background knowledge prior to reading, which will affect comprehension

3. ability to make specific predictions

4. ability to read phrased chunks of text

5. discrepancy between oral and silent reading comprehension

6. ability to retell

7. ability to sequence

8. ability to respond accurately to comprehension questions

To make the informal reading inventories most beneficial for guiding your instruction, it is very important that they are done in their entirety. If any part is skipped, then your knowledge about the student's reading fluency is incomplete. Future instruction should be strategy based—not level based. Therefore, it is important to know which strategy to teach (e.g., retelling, sequencing, phrasing).

Each reading selection is based on a fifth-grade reading level. Remember that there is often a discrepancy between a fifth grader's ability to comprehend fiction and nonfiction text. Most students comprehend fiction text at least one grade level (usually two) higher than their comprehension level of nonfiction text. Since a goal of fifth-grade reading is to help students make better use of the nonfiction text they read, the reading selections in this book are more heavily weighted toward nonfiction text.

Forms A and B focus on early fifth-grade reading, while Forms C and D focus on later fifth-grade reading. This gives you the opportunity to reassess a student throughout the year.

Scoring Goals

Average fifth-grade oral reading rates:
(in words correctly read per minute)

%ile	Fall	Winter	Spring
75	126	143	151
50	105	118	128
25	77	93	100

Comprehension questions: 6–8

Retelling: sequenced, oral, and silent, 70% of what was read

Sequencing: beginning to end

Goal for fifth graders in phrasing: 3- to 5-word phrases depending on meaningful chunking

Directions for administering the Informal Reading Inventory to one student:

1. In advance, photocopy the student text version of the form you choose from pages 13 and 14. Cut along the dotted lines so the student only sees the text he or she will read. Get a timer.

2. Ask the student the background knowledge questions. Quickly take notes on his or her responses.

3. Tell the student the title of the reading selection. Tell him or her that the background questions are related. Ask the student to make a prediction. Write down what he or she says. (Watch for students who simply rephrase the title. That is not a prediction and indicates a need for direct instruction in making predictions using known information.)

4. Tell the student he or she will be reading the first half aloud to you so you can hear his or her reading. Tell the student that he or she will read the rest of the selection silently.

5. Start the timer when the student is ready. As the student reads, mark the exact phrases (or words) read using the following notations:

$\sim\!\!\sim\!\!\sim$ = the phrases read

✓ = one word read (not a phrase)

◯ = error that changes the meaning of the sentence

_____ = error that preserves meaning of original sentence

6. Stop the timer when the student reaches the end of the oral reading paragraph. Record this amount of time. Tell the student to continue reading silently. Start the timer. When the student is finished, stop the timer, and record this silent reading time.

7. Ask the student to tell you everything he or she remembered.

8. As the student retells the information recalled, you will be numbering the blanks in the retelling section to reflect the order in which the information was recalled. The numbers (versus check marks) are important because they will tell you the student's sequential recall level.
- Watch to see if the student first tells you something that he or she had as incorrect background knowledge. That is evidence of a student who did not read to learn.
- Watch for the student who recalls the last bit of information first and then goes backward. That indicates a powerful recency effect for that child.
- Watch for the student who only cites unrelated details without combining them into main ideas.

9. Ask the student the comprehension questions. Record the student's responses.

10. Calculate the words per minute. The circled number at the end of each reading selection indicates the number of words in that selection.
- Calculate Words Read Correctly: # of words read _____ – errors = words read correctly
- Calculate Words per Minute (WPM): # of words read correctly ____ x 60 ÷ # seconds to read the passage = _____ (WPM)

11. Send the student back to his or her activities and immediately analyze the information. This will help you target exactly what that student needs first.

Analyzing the Information You Recorded

1. Look at the student's background knowledge and his or her sequenced retelling.
- Did the student correct a misconception? If so, the student made connections between the print and previous assumptions.
- Did the student have limited background knowledge? Analyze how that related to responses. In the fifth grade, students should be able to read and learn with limited prior knowledge.

2. Look at the student's prediction.
- Did the student restate the title as a prediction? If so, the student does not use known information to form predictions; a mini-lesson will be necessary.
- Did the student tie in other background knowledge? If so, the student is ready to learn from text.

3. Look at the number of decoding errors you marked. What do they have in common?
- Did the student read words incorrectly and keep going? If so, then no meaning was used, and the student needs a mini-lesson on how to monitor his or her comprehension.
- Did the student struggle with multisyllabic words? If so, the student needs help with breaking words into chunks.

4. Look at the phrased chunks you marked.
- Did the student read word by word (mostly check marks) or in phrases? If the student read word by word, then he or she requires individual direct fluency instruction. If the phrased chunks are consistently less than four-word phrases, then the activities in this book should be used in small groups or individualized based on the length of the phrases and the level of comprehension.

5. Look at the length of time it took the student to read orally and silently. Which is faster? Now go straight to the retelling.
- Did the student retell more information orally or silently? If you see a discrepancy, then you have identified a student who comprehends better at this point either orally or silently. (Usually, the difference shows that the student has higher oral comprehension than silent. This student needs to be able to do all independent reading while reading aloud in a whisper voice.)

6. Look at the retelling. The ability to retell without prompts is a higher level of comprehension than answering questions that aid recall.
- Did the student retell in order? This student has a good sequential memory.
- Did the student retell backward? The recency effect was in place.
- Did the student bounce around with details? If so, the student needs a mini-lesson on recalling information in sequence.
- Did the student retell only what was read orally? This student does not comprehend well when reading silently. All classroom reading should involve reading aloud for that student.
- Did the student retell the numerical information first? This indicates a good visual memory.

7. Look at the comprehension questions.
- Did the student recall only explicit information? This student is literal in reading and needs a mini-lesson on making connections to text, elaborations, and inferences—thinking beyond the reading.
- Did the student miss most of the questions? Look at the phrasing ability. Often, this student is suffering from a lack of fluency.

Wolves

Wolves are the largest members of the canine family. In the United States they must share space with human beings. If wolves are not protected, they may become an endangered species.

Many adults think wolves pose a threat to their farm animals. Actually, most livestock die from disease. Wolves do have an effect on wildlife in the United States, but it is a good one. They leave dead elk and deer for other animals to eat. Eagles and bears are two animals that have more to eat when wolves are around. Wolves also keep the coyote population from growing too large. Foxes can come back now that there are fewer coyotes in the area.

Recently, family packs of wolves were brought to Yellowstone Park from Canada. The instinct to go home is so strong in wolves that the packs traveled 30 miles north toward Canada. Then, they realized that they did not know how to go home. The wolves returned to the place where they were released. They began to hunt the elk and deer that live there. They produced many litters of wolf pups and spread out through the park. The sound of wolf howls returned to the park.

Have wolves benefited human beings in other ways? Yes. They attract tourists. The tourists spend millions of dollars at the businesses around Yellowstone. The reintroduction of wolves to the park is a success.

Volcanoes

A volcano can be on land or under water. It can be a hole in the ground that lava comes through. It can be a mountain formed by lava as it hardens. Under Earth's crust is hot, melted rock called magma. When the magma pushes up through Earth's crust, it forms a volcano. Magma is called lava when it comes out into the air.

Not all volcanoes erupt. An inactive volcano is called dormant. Dormant volcanoes are good for plants. Rich soil created by ancient eruptions provides good habitats for wildlife. Active volcanoes could erupt at anytime. Some eruptions continue for years. Other eruptions only last for hours.

An eruption can create land. Active volcanoes in the Pacific Ocean formed the islands of Hawaii. They are still active today. Old lava flows make good soil. They help beautiful plants grow all over the islands. Many people visit the islands just to see the volcanoes. Scientists live there and study the volcanoes to learn more about them.

Volcanoes may destroy land, too. Many thousands of years ago, people lived on an island near modern Greece. They were called the Minoans. They were known for the boats they built and the pottery they made. When the volcano in the middle of their island paradise erupted, it caused the island to sink. Many people had already escaped from the island, but the culture did not survive without its home. The Minoans disappeared after their volcanic island home was destroyed.

Jaguars

The jaguar is the largest cat in the Americas. Jaguars are found in Central and South America. They are found in swamps or thick forests with access to water. Jaguars are carnivores, or meat eaters, so they prey upon other animals to survive. They eat a wide variety of animals. They eat snakes, deer, mice, river turtles, and more.

Today jaguars are protected under the Endangered Species Act. It is illegal to hunt or harm them. In the past, they were hunted for their beautiful spotted fur. Today, their biggest danger is a loss of space to live. The jaguar's only natural enemy is man.

Jaguars are sometimes mistaken for the leopard since they both have spots. However, the spots of a jaguar have dots in the middle and are larger than the leopard's spots. Jaguars also have shorter legs and bulkier bodies.

When seen in the wild, a jaguar is usually near the water. Jaguars like the water and are great swimmers. National parks that protect jaguars often provide habitats with this in mind. Jaguars are most populous in the rainforests of South America. This is related to the fact that much of the rainforest is protected from being destroyed. There are fewer humans. The goal is for the jaguar to continue to survive in the wild.

Tornado Alley

A tornado is a kind of windstorm. It is often part of a thunderstorm. Tornadoes occur all over the world, but they are most common in the United States. A tornado is a column of spinning air. It creates updrafts that can lift things off the ground, spin them around, and then drop them back on the ground. A tornado can do a lot of damage.

Most tornadoes occur in the middle states. Tornado Alley is an area where most tornadoes occur each year. It stretches from northern Texas through the Dakotas. People who live in the area practice tornado safety often. Radios broadcast tornado warnings so people can be prepared.

Tornado Alley includes ten states. Texas has the most tornadoes because it is so big. Hundreds of violent storms pass through the area each year. Luckily, most tornadoes occur over areas where few people live, so they do less damage when they touch down.

The geography of the central states creates spring and summer thunderstorms called super cells. Warm, humid air from the Gulf of Mexico collides with cooler, drier air from Canada. When these air masses meet, they create huge thunderstorms. As a result, there are often tornadoes. The flat lands of this region allow fast-moving winds in the lower atmosphere. These winds also make tornadoes more likely.

Developing Reading Fluency • Gr. 5 © 2004 Creative Teaching Press

Name _____   Date _____

Wolves

Background Questions

What animals are related to wolves? _____ known/unknown

Where do wolves eat? _____ known/unknown

What is an endangered species? _____ known/unknown

What do you know about wolves? _____ known/unknown

Prediction

What do you think you will learn when you read this selection called *Wolves?*

_____

_____

Decoding and Fluency

Wolves are the largest members of the canine family. In the United States they must share space with human beings. If wolves are not protected, they may become an endangered species.

Many adults think wolves pose a threat to their farm animals. Actually, most livestock die from disease. Wolves do have an effect on wildlife in the United States, but it is a good one. They leave dead elk and deer for other animals to eat. Eagles and bears are two animals that have more to eat when wolves are around. Wolves also keep the coyote population from growing too large. Foxes can come back now that there are fewer coyotes in the area.

(114) | **Oral reading time:** | | errors | | **meaning-changing errors**

Recently, family packs of wolves were brought to Yellowstone Park from Canada. The instinct to go home is so strong in wolves that the packs traveled 30 miles north towards Canada. Then, they realized that they did not know how to go home. The wolves returned to the place where they were released. They began to hunt the elk and deer that live there. They produced many litters of wolf pups and spread out through the park. The sound of wolf howls returned to the park.

Have wolves benefited human beings in other ways? Yes. They attract tourists. The tourists spend millions of dollars at the businesses around Yellowstone. The reintroduction of wolves to the park is a success.

(117) | **Silent reading time:** |

Developing Reading Fluency • Gr. 5 © 2004 Creative Teaching Press

Informal Reading Inventories

Name _____   Date _____

Scoring Form

Reading Rate ORAL SILENT **WPM =** _____ **WPM =** _____ **Expression:** yes no **Read punctuation:** yes no	**Phrasing** (look at swoops and check marks) _____ word by word _____ some words and some 2-word phrases _____ mostly 2-word phrases _____ 2- and 3-word phrases _____ 3- and 4-word phrases _____ phrases of 4 or more words consistently

Retelling: "Tell me everything you read and learned about wolves."

ORAL	**SILENT**
_____ largest members of the canine family _____ share space with human beings _____ may become an endangered species _____ belief that wolves pose threat to farm animals _____ most livestock die from disease _____ wolves have good effect on wildlife _____ leave dead elk and deer for other animals to eat _____ eagles and bears have more to eat _____ keep the coyote population from growing too large _____ foxes can come back	_____ family packs brought to Yellowstone _____ strong instinct to go home _____ packs traveled 30 miles north toward Canada _____ realized they did not know how to go home _____ returned to release location _____ began to hunt elk and deer _____ produced many litters of wolf pups _____ spread out through the park _____ sound of wolf howls returned to park _____ attract tourists _____ tourists spend millions of dollars at the businesses around Yellowstone _____ reintroduction to the park is a success

Discrepancy between oral and silent?   yes   no   (circle one)

Sequenced?   beg. to end   end to beg.   random   (circle one)

Comprehension questions: (Look for questions already answered in retelling.)

Explicit (in the text)

_____ **1.** What species competes with wolves for land? **ORAL** (human beings)

_____ **2.** What is the leading cause of death to livestock? **ORAL** (disease)

_____ **3.** Where did the first pack reintroduced to Yellowstone come from? **SILENT** (Canada)

_____ **4.** Which animals benefit from wolves? **SILENT** (eagles, bears, foxes, people)

Implicit (inferences, elaborations, making connections)

_____ **5.** What do you think visitors to the park are hoping to see or hear? (wolf howls, cubs playing, pack traveling together)

_____ **6.** How might knowing that wolves have a strong instinct to go home reassure people? (know wolves won't leave Yellowstone)

_____ **7.** Why do you think organizations try to help the wolves? (various answers)

_____ **8.** What else do you think belongs in the canine family? (answers could include dogs)

8 = independent   **6 or 7 = instructional**   **5 or less = too challenging**   **Total** _____

Developing Reading Fluency • Gr. 5 © 2004 Creative Teaching Press

Volcanoes

Background Questions

What comes out of a volcano? _____ known/unknown

What good things happen when volcanoes erupt? _____ known/unknown

What bad things happen when volcanoes erupt?_____ known/unknown

What else do you know about volcanoes? _____ known/unknown

Prediction

What do you think you will learn when you read this selection called *Volcanoes?*

_____

_____

Decoding and Fluency

A volcano can be on land or under water. It can be a hole in the ground that lava comes through. It can be a mountain formed by lava as it hardens. Under Earth's crust is hot, melted rock called magma. When the magma pushes up through Earth's crust, it forms a volcano. Magma is called lava when it comes out into the air.

Not all volcanoes erupt. An inactive volcano is called dormant. Dormant volcanoes are good for plants. Rich soil created by ancient eruptions provides good habitats for wildlife. Active volcanoes could erupt at anytime. Some eruptions continue for years. Other eruptions only last for hours.

(108) | **Oral reading time:** | | errors | | **meaning-changing errors**

An eruption can create land. Active volcanoes in the Pacific Ocean formed the islands of Hawaii. They are still active today. Old lava flows make good soil. They help beautiful plants grow all over the islands. Many people visit the islands just to see the volcanoes. Scientists live there and study the volcanoes to learn more about them.

Volcanoes may destroy land, too. Many thousands of years ago, people lived on an island near modern Greece. They were called the Minoans. They were known for the boats they built and the pottery they made. When the volcano in the middle of their island paradise erupted, it caused the island to sink. Many people had already escaped the island, but the culture did not survive without its home. The Minoans disappeared after their volcanic island home was destroyed.

(138) | **Silent reading time:** |

Name _____ Date _____

Scoring Form

Reading Rate

ORAL	SILENT
WPM = _____	WPM = _____

Expression: yes   no

Read punctuation: yes   no

Phrasing
(look at swoops and check marks)

_____ word by word
_____ some words and some 2-word phrases
_____ mostly 2-word phrases
_____ 2- and 3-word phrases
_____ 3- and 4-word phrases
_____ phrases of 4 or more words consistently

Retelling: "Tell me everything you read and learned about volcanoes."

ORAL

_____ a volcano can be on land or under water
_____ can be a hole in the ground that lava comes through
_____ can be a mountain formed by lava
_____ under Earth's crust is magma
_____ when magma pushes up through Earth's crust, it forms a volcano
_____ magma is called lava when it comes out into the air
_____ not all volcanoes erupt
_____ inactive volcano called dormant
_____ dormant volcanoes are good for plants
_____ rich soil provides good habitats for wildlife
_____ active volcanoes could erupt at anytime
_____ some eruptions continue for years
_____ other eruptions only last for hours

SILENT

_____ an eruption can create land
_____ active volcanoes in Pacific formed Hawaii
_____ Hawaiian volcanoes still active
_____ old lava flows make good soil
_____ help beautiful plants grow
_____ people visit just to see volcanoes
_____ scientists study volcanoes
_____ volcanoes may destroy land
_____ Minoans lived on an island near Greece
_____ known for boats and pottery
_____ volcano in middle of island erupted
_____ caused island to sink
_____ many people had already escaped
_____ Minoans disappeared after island home destroyed

Discrepancy between oral and silent?   yes   no   (circle one)

Sequenced?   beg. to end   end to beg.   random   (circle one)

Comprehension questions: (Look for questions already answered in retelling.)

Explicit (in the text)

_____ **1.** Name two regions where volcanoes are found. **ORAL** (on land, under water)
_____ **2.** What is magma called when comes in contact with air? **ORAL** (lava)
_____ **3.** Which ancient civilization was ended when a volcano erupted? **SILENT** (Minoan)
_____ **4.** Name a U.S. state formed by volcanoes. **SILENT** (Hawaii)

Implicit (inferences, elaborations, making connections)

_____ **5.** How is a volcano different from a regular mountain? (regular mountain has no lava)
_____ **6.** What is the difference between active and dormant volcanoes? (comparison)
_____ **7.** Why might some villages be close to volcanoes? (rich soil, trees, wildlife, dormant)
_____ **8.** Why are the volcanoes on the Hawaiian islands popular vacation spots? (various answers)

8 = independent   6 or 7 = instructional   5 or less = too challenging   **Total** _____

Developing Reading Fluency • Gr. 5 © 2004 Creative Teaching Press

Jaguars

Background Questions

What is a jaguar? _____ known/unknown

Where do jaguars live? _____ known/unknown

What is an endangered species? _____ known/unknown

What else do you know about jaguars? _____ known/unknown

Prediction

What do you think you will learn when you read this selection called *Jaguars?*

_____

_____

Decoding and Fluency

The jaguar is the largest cat in the Americas. Jaguars are found in Central and South America. They are found in swamps or thick forests with access to water. Jaguars are carnivores, or meat eaters, so they prey upon other animals to survive. They eat a wide variety of animals. They eat snakes, deer, mice, river turtles, and more.

Today jaguars are protected under the Endangered Species Act. It is illegal to hunt or harm them. In the past, they were hunted for their beautiful spotted fur. Today, their biggest danger is a loss of space to live. The jaguar's only natural enemy is man.

(107) | **Oral reading time:** | | **errors** | | **meaning-changing errors**

Jaguars are sometimes mistaken for the leopard since they both have spots. However, the spots of a jaguar have dots in the middle and are larger than the leopard's spots. Jaguars also have shorter legs and bulkier bodies.

When seen in the wild, a jaguar is usually near the water. Jaguars like the water and are great swimmers. National parks that protect jaguars often provide habitats with this in mind. Jaguars are most populous in the rainforests of South America. This is related to the fact that much of the rainforest is protected from being destroyed. There are fewer humans. The goal is for the jaguar to continue to survive in the wild.

(112) | **Silent reading time:** |

Name _____   Date _____

Scoring Form

Reading Rate	Phrasing
ORAL **SILENT**	(look at swoops and check marks)
WPM = _____ **WPM =** _____	_____ word by word
Expression: yes no	_____ some words and some 2-word phrases
Read punctuation: yes no	_____ mostly 2-word phrases
	_____ 2- and 3-word phrases
	_____ 3- and 4-word phrases
	_____ phrases of 4 or more words consistently

Retelling: "Tell me everything you read and learned about jaguars."

ORAL	SILENT
_____ jaguar is the largest cat in the Americas	_____ people confuse the jaguar with the leopard
_____ found in Central and South America	_____ both have spots
_____ found in swamps or thick forests with access to water	_____ spots are different
_____ are carnivores	_____ spots of a jaguar are larger
_____ prey upon other animals to survive	_____ with dots in the middle
_____ eat a wide variety of animals	_____ jaguars have shorter legs
_____ eat snakes, deer, mice, river turtles	_____ and bulkier bodies
_____ protected by Endangered Species Act	_____ in the wild, a jaguar is usually near water
_____ illegal to hunt or harm the jaguars	_____ like water
_____ hunted for their beautiful spotted fur	_____ great swimmers
_____ biggest danger is a loss of space to live	_____ national parks that protect jaguars
_____ only natural enemy is man	_____ provide habitats with water
	_____ found in the rainforests of South America
	_____ much of the rainforest land is protected
	_____ fewer humans
	_____ goal for jaguars to survive in the wild

Discrepancy between oral and silent?   yes   no   (circle one)

Sequenced?   beg. to end   end to beg.   random   (circle one)

Comprehension questions: (Look for questions already answered in retelling.)

Explicit (in the text)

_____ **1.** What do jaguars eat? **ORAL** (meat, other animals)

_____ **2.** What protects the jaguars today? **ORAL** (Endangered Species Act)

_____ **3.** What is unusual about jaguars (as cats)? **SILENT** (love water, swim)

_____ **4.** Which part of the world has the largest population of jaguars? **SILENT** (S. America)

Implicit (inferences, elaborations, making connections)

_____ **5.** Why is the jaguar in danger of disappearing forever? (hunters, no land)

_____ **6.** How are jaguars and leopards different? (comparison)

_____ **7.** Why were jaguars put on the Endangered Species List? (stop hunting, give land)

_____ **8.** If you could design a jaguar habitat, what would it look like? Describe it. (various answers)

8 = independent   **6 or 7 = instructional**   **5 or less = too challenging**   **Total** _____

Developing Reading Fluency • Gr. 5 © 2004 Creative Teaching Press

Tornado Alley

Background Questions

What is an alley? _____ known/unknown

What causes a tornado? _____ known/unknown

Where do most tornadoes occur? _____ known/unknown

What else do you know about tornadoes? _____ known/unknown

Prediction

What do you think you will learn when you read this selection called *Tornado Alley?*

_____

_____

Decoding and Fluency

A tornado is a kind of windstorm. It is often part of a thunderstorm. Tornadoes occur all over the world, but they are most common in the United States. A tornado is a column of spinning air. It creates updrafts that can lift things off the ground, spin them around, and then drop them back on the ground. A tornado can do a lot of damage.

Most tornadoes occur in the middle states. Tornado Alley is an area where most tornadoes occur each year. It stretches from northern Texas through the Dakotas. People who live in the area practice tornado safety often. Radios broadcast tornado warnings so people can be prepared.

(111) | **Oral reading time:** | | errors | | **meaning-changing errors**

Tornado Alley includes ten states. Texas has the most tornadoes because it is so big. Hundreds of violent storms pass through the area each year. Luckily, most tornadoes occur over areas where few people live, so they do less damage when they touch down.

The geography of the central states creates spring and summer thunderstorms called super cells. Warm, humid air from the Gulf of Mexico collides with cooler, drier air from Canada. When these air masses meet, they create huge thunderstorms. As a result, there are often tornadoes. The flat lands of this region allow fast-moving winds in the lower atmosphere. These winds also make tornadoes more likely.

(110) | **Silent reading time:** |

Name _____   Date _____

Reading Rate		**Phrasing**

Reading Rate

ORAL   SILENT

WPM = _____   WPM = _____

Expression: yes   no

Read punctuation: yes   no

Phrasing

(look at swoops and check marks)

_____ word by word

_____ some words and some 2-word phrases

_____ mostly 2-word phrases

_____ 2- and 3-word phrases

_____ 3- and 4-word phrases

_____ phrases of 4 or more words consistently

Retelling: "Tell me everything you read and learned about Tornado Alley."

ORAL

_____ a kind of windstorm

_____ part of a thunderstorm

_____ occur all over the world

_____ most common in the United States

_____ column of spinning air

_____ creates updrafts that

_____ lift things off the ground

_____ spin them around

_____ drop them back on the ground

_____ can do a lot of damage

_____ most occur in the middle states

_____ Tornado Alley where most occur

_____ from Texas through the Dakotas

_____ people practice tornado safety

_____ radios broadcast warnings

SILENT

_____ Texas has most tornadoes because it is big

_____ hundreds of violent storms each year

_____ most tornadoes occur where few people live

_____ they do less damage

_____ central states geography creates

_____ spring and summer thunderstorms

_____ called super cells

_____ warm, humid air from Gulf of Mexico

_____ collides with

_____ cooler, drier air from Canada

_____ huge thunderstorms take place

_____ result in tornadoes

_____ flat lands allow fast-moving winds in the lower atmosphere

_____ winds also make tornados more likely

Discrepancy between oral and silent?   yes   no   (circle one)

Sequenced?   beg. to end   end to beg.   random   (circle one)

Comprehension questions: (Look for questions already answered in retelling.)

Explicit (in the text)

_____ **1.** A tornado is part of a _____. **ORAL** (thunderstorm)

_____ **2.** Where is Tornado Alley? **ORAL** (middle states—Texas to Dakotas)

_____ **3.** How does a tornado form? **SILENT** (warm air mass meets a cooler air mass)

_____ **4.** Huge thunderstorms are called _____. **ORAL** (super cells)

Implicit (inferences, elaborations, making connections)

_____ **5.** How is a tornado worse than a regular thunderstorm? (comparison details)

_____ **6.** When would be the worst time to plan a trip to Texas if you didn't want to see a tornado? (spring or summer)

_____ **7.** Where could you live to avoid frequent tornados? Why? (identify a location other than the Great Plains states)

_____ **8.** Why do people need to practice tornado safety? (fast winds, pick things up, violent)

8 = independent   6 or 7 = instructional   5 or less = too challenging   **Total** _____

Developing Reading Fluency • Gr. 5 © 2004 Creative Teaching Press

Read-Arounds

According to research, one reason why students do not read with phrasing and fluency is that they do not have a solid base of high-frequency words and sight words, which is required for reading books independently. Research recommends activities that give students practice with frequently used words. This will in turn help with phrasing and fluency because students will not need to slow down to decode as often. The Read-Around cards in this section are already written in phrases (spaces between groups of words), so students can see and better understand how to read words in groups. The Read-Around cards are designed for groups of two to four students. This allows for optimal amounts of practice and active involvement. The phrases on the cards are short and simple to help students focus directly on reading phrases and practicing high-frequency and content words.

Strategies: phrased reading; repeated oral reading; active listening; reading high-frequency, content, and sight words

Materials
- construction paper or tagboard
- envelopes
- scissors

Directions

1. Choose a set of cards (e.g., idioms, proverbs), and copy the cards on construction paper or tagboard. (Each set of cards is two pages.) Cut apart the cards, and laminate them so that they can be reused throughout the school year. Put the cards in an envelope, and write the title (e.g., *Exploration*) on the envelope.

2. Give a set of cards to a small group of students so that each student has three to six cards. Review with students the pronunciation and meaning of the bold words and phrases on their clue cards so that they are familiar and comfortable with them (or preteach the words).

3. Explain that students will play a listening and reading game. Model how the game works and share the correct answers with each group the first time students play using a new set of cards. Read aloud each student's cards, and then have students silently read their cards at least five times to build fluency. Discuss each question and corresponding answer so students can concentrate more on reading fluently than on determining the answer to the question as they play.

4. Tell the group that the student who has the clue card that says *I have the first card* will begin the game by reading aloud his or her card. Then, have the student with the answer to the clue read aloud his or he card. Tell students to continue until they get back to the first card. (The game ends after a student reads *Who has the first card?* and a student answers *I have the first card.*)

5. Encourage students to play the game at least twice. Have students shuffle and deal the cards again so that students read different cards each time.

Extension

Invite students to take home a set of cards. Have them teach their families how to play and practice reading the cards with family members. Encourage families to make additional cards.

Idioms

I have   the first card.

Who has the meaning   of the idiom in

"I am **up to my ears**   in paperwork!"

I have the meaning   that you have

a ton of paperwork   that you need to finish.

Who has the meaning   of the idiom in

"Our teacher   **has eyes**   **in the back**   **of her head!**"

I have the meaning   that you **notice**

that our teacher   always knows   what's going on.

Who has the meaning   of the idiom in

"Dad was **keeping**   **a close eye**   on the pot of water   on the stove."

I have the meaning   that Dad is **carefully watching**

the pot of water   so that it doesn't   boil over.

Who has the meaning   of the idiom in

"The baby cried out   with an **ear-splitting** scream."

I have the meaning   that the baby

was screaming so loudly   that it hurt your ears.

Who has the meaning   of the idiom in

"There was simply no   **elbow room**   at the dinner table."

I have the meaning   that the table   was too crowded!

Who has the meaning   of the idiom in

"It's a surprise party,   **so keep it under your hat.**"

Developing Reading Fluency • Gr. 5 © 2004 Creative Teaching Press

Idioms

I have the meaning   that you have to keep it   a big secret.
Who has the meaning   of the idiom in
"She told me   to **make myself at home.**"

I have the meaning   that you were told   to feel comfortable.
Who has the meaning   of the idiom in
"I need more than an umbrella.   **It's raining cats and dogs!**"

I have the meaning   that the rain is coming down
so hard   that an umbrella   is not enough!
Who has the meaning   of the idiom in
"I need to **brush up**   **on** my history."

I have the meaning   that you need to study history.
Who has the meaning   of the idiom in   "Is he **up to something?**"

I have the meaning   that you think
he is doing something   that he should not.
Who has the meaning   of the idiom in
"Sometimes we don't   **see eye to eye.**"

I have the meaning   that you don't always agree.
Who has the first card?

Developing Reading Fluency • Gr. 5 © 2004 Creative Teaching Press

Proverbs

I have   the first card.

Who has the meaning   of this proverb?

"Birds of a feather   flock together."

I have the meaning   that people   often judge you

by the friends you choose   to spend time with.

Who has the meaning   of this proverb?

"Actions speak   louder than words."

I have the meaning   that what you do

means more   than what you say.

Who has the meaning   of this proverb?

"Two wrongs   don't make a right."

I have the meaning   that if someone   does something wrong

to you,   doing something wrong   **in return**   will not make things better.

Who has the meaning   of this proverb?

"An ounce of prevention   is worth a pound of cure."

I have the meaning   that it is better   to prevent a bad **situation**

than to try   to fix the **consequences** later.

Who has the meaning   of this proverb?

"Don't count your chickens   before they hatch."

I have the meaning   that you should not make plans

based on something   that has not happened yet.

Who has the meaning   of this proverb?

"Many hands make light work."

Developing Reading Fluency • Gr. 5 © 2004 Creative Teaching Press

Proverbs

I have the meaning   that teamwork   makes any job easier.
Who has the meaning   of this proverb?
"All work and no play   makes Jack a dull boy."

I have the meaning   that it is good to work hard,
but you still need   to make time to have fun.
Who has the meaning   of this proverb?
"Look before you leap."

I have the meaning   that you should think   about the results
before you decide   to do something.
Who has the meaning   of this proverb?
"Beauty is only skin deep."

I have the meaning   that what is most important   in a person
is on the inside   not the outside.
Who has the meaning   of this proverb?
"What goes around,   comes around."

I have the meaning   that people will treat you
the way   that you treat them.
Who has the meaning   of this proverb?
"Every cloud has   a silver lining."

I have the meaning   that everything bad   has some good in it.
Who has the first card?

Geography 101

I have   the first card.

Who has the name   of the zero line   of **latitude**

where temperatures   are the warmest?

I have the equator.

Who has the name   of a piece of land

that's surrounded by water   on all sides?

I have an island.

Who has the name   of the large ocean   located off the

east coast of the Americas   where most hurricanes form?

I have the Atlantic Ocean.

Who has the name   of the major river   in the United States

that formed   the Grand Canyon?

I have the Colorado River.

Who has the name   of a narrow waterway

that connects   two bodies of water?

I have a **strait.**

Who has the word   that is a waterway   dug across land

for transportation or irrigation?

Developing Reading Fluency • Gr. 5 © 2004 Creative Teaching Press

Geography 101

I have a canal.

Who has the name   of the smallest state   in the United States?

I have Rhode Island.

Who has the name   of this mountain range

where the **Continental Divide**   is located?

I have the Rocky Mountains.

Who has the name   of the major gulf

found off the southern coast   of the United States?

I have   the Gulf of Mexico.

Who has the name   of a book of maps?

I have an atlas.

Who has the name   of the five major lakes   shared by

the United States and Canada?

I have   the Great Lakes.

Who has the first card?

Developing Reading Fluency • Gr. 5 © 2004 Creative Teaching Press

Read-Arounds

Exploration

I have   the first card.
Who has the name   of the group of explorers   who sailed
from Norway, Iceland, or Greenland   to North America   around A.D. 1000?

I have the Vikings.
Who has the name   of the nation   that paid for
the voyages   of Christopher Columbus   and was ruled
by King Ferdinand   and Queen Isabella?

I have Spain.
Who has the name   of the Spanish explorer
who conquered   the Aztecs?

I have Hernando Cortes.
Who has the names   of the three ships
that sailed   in the 1492 voyage   of Columbus?

I have   the Niña, Pinta, and Santa Maria.
Who has the name   of the cloth
the Europeans wanted   to get from China?

I have silk.
Who has the name   of the instrument or tool   used by sailors
that told them   which direction   they were headed?

Developing Reading Fluency • Gr. 5 © 2004 Creative Teaching Press

Exploration

I have a compass.
Who has the name of the route to Asia through North America that some early explorers were searching for?

I have the Northwest Passage.
Who has the name of the continent on which the ancient Inca civilization once stood?

I have South America.
Who has the name of a settlement of people who left their own country for another land?

I have a colony.
Who has the name of a person who makes maps?

I have a cartographer.
Who has the name of the island off the coast of North America that was named by John Cabot?

I have Newfoundland.
Who has the first card?

Developing Reading Fluency • Gr. 5 © 2004 Creative Teaching Press

Measurement 101

I have the first card.

Who has the distance   you measure   around the outside
of an object   by finding the sum   of the lengths   of its sides?

I have   the perimeter of the object.

Who has the space   inside an object   found by multiplying
the length by the width   of the object?

I have   the area of the object.
Who has the number   of feet in a mile?

I have 5,280 feet.
Who has the number   of centimeters in a meter?

I have 100 centimeters.
Who has the number   of grams in a **kilogram?**

I have 1,000 grams.
Who has the number   of **ounces** in a cup?

Developing Reading Fluency • Gr. 5 © 2004 Creative Teaching Press

Measurement 101

I have 8 fluid ounces.

Who has the number   of pints in a gallon?

I have 8 pints.

Who has the number   of ounces in a pint?

I have 16 fluid ounces.

Who has the number   of cups in a pint?

I have 2 cups.

Who has the number   of inches in a yard?

I have 36 inches.

Who has the number   of meters in a **decameter?**

I have 10 meters.

Who has the first card?

Algebra Ah-ha's

I have the first card.
Remember that "n" represents "a number."
Who has a number decreased by ten?

I have $n - 10$.
Who has the sum of nine and a number?

I have $n + 9$.
Who has a number subtracted from nine?

I have $9 - n$.
Who has the **product** of seven and a number?

I have $7n$.
Who has a number added to 27 ?

I have $27 + n$.
Who has the **quotient** of 35 and a number?

I have $35 \div n$.
Who has five times the sum of a number and three?

I have $5(n + 3)$.
Who has 27 times a number?

I have $27n$.
Who has 35 more than a number?

Developing Reading Fluency • Gr. 5 © 2004 Creative Teaching Press

Algebra Ah-ha's

I have $n + 35$.

Who has three times   the difference   between a number and 12?

I have $3(12 - n)$.

Who has nine less   than the product of five   and some number?

I have $5n - 9$.

Who has four more   than the product of two   and some number?

I have $2n + 4$.

Who has the sum   of some number and 12?

I have $n + 12$.

Who has the product   of 12 and some number?

I have $12n$.

Who has a number   subtracted from three dozen?

I have $36 - n$.

Who has nine sets   of a number?

I have $9n$.

Who has a number   multiplied by 7?

I have $7n$.

Who has the first card?

Developing Reading Fluency • Gr. 5 © 2004 Creative Teaching Press

Science 101

I have the first card.

Who has the name   of the layer of air

that surrounds   our planet Earth?

I have the atmosphere.

Who has the name   of an animal

that does not   have a backbone?

I have an **invertebrate.**

Who has the name   of an intense windstorm

that forms over land   often as part of   a severe thunderstorm?

I have a tornado.

Who has the name   of the layer   of Earth's atmosphere

which is the hottest   and farthest   from the planet's surface?

I have the **thermosphere.**

Who has the name   of the smallest unit   of an element

that has all of the properties   of that element?

I have an atom.

Who has the name   of the instrument or tool

used to measure   wind air temperature?

Developing Reading Fluency • Gr. 5 © 2004 Creative Teaching Press

Science 101

I have a thermometer.
Who has the name   of the basic unit of **structure** and **function**
of all living things?

I have the cell.
Who has the name   of the stage   in the water cycle
when the liquid   changes into a gas?

I have evaporation.
Who has the name   of the large, spiraling storm system
that has high winds,   begins over water,   and can reach speeds of 74 mph?

I have a hurricane.
Who has the name   of the type of winds   that are global
and blow constantly   from the same direction?

I have the prevailing winds.
Who has the name   of the weight   of particles of air
pressing down on Earth's surface?

I have air pressure.
Who has the first card?

Read-Arounds

Parts of Speech

I have the first card.

Who has the name | of the part of speech | that describes a noun?

I have an adjective.

Who has the name | of the part of speech | that describes
a verb, an adverb, or an adjective?

I have an adverb.

Who has the name | of the part of speech | that joins and connects
words, phrases, or clauses?

I have a conjunction.

Who has the name | of the part of speech | that is a word
expressing strong emotion | in a sentence such as | "Help! I'm lost!"

I have an interjection.

Who has the name | of the part of speech | that is a person,
place, thing, or idea, | and can be common or proper?

I have a noun.

Who has the name | of the part of speech | that relates
a noun or pronoun | to another part of the sentence?
Some examples include | *at, by, in, to, from,* | *under, with,* and *since.*

Developing Reading Fluency • Gr. 5 © 2004 Creative Teaching Press

Parts of Speech

I have a preposition.

Who has the name   of the part of speech   that replaces a noun?
Some examples include   *me, you, I, we,*   *she, he,* and *us.*

I have a pronoun.

Who has the name   of the part of speech   that includes
all of the words   that show action?

I have an action verb.

Who has the name   that labels   the words *a, an,* and *the*?

I have an article.

Who has the name   of a word or phrase   in a sentence
that refers to the person or thing   receiving the action of a verb?

I have a direct object.

Who has the name   of the part of speech   that describes
how one noun   compares to another?

I have a comparative adjective.
Who has the first card?

Developing Reading Fluency • Gr. 5 © 2004 Creative Teaching Press

Read-Arounds

Phrasing Fun

Students who are still not reading with phrasing and fluency will have a difficult time with the transition from learning to read to reading to learn. This skill is critical by the fifth grade for middle-school success due to the link between phrasing and comprehension. If a student is still focusing on the decoding process of the text, then he or she is unable to focus on the meaning behind the words he or she is busy decoding. This impedes the comprehension process and breaks down learning. These students need many opportunities to listen to phrasing and practice reading phrased chunks of between three and five words. They must transfer this practice into ongoing text. The fun, motivating activities in this section put the emphasis on meaning rather than decoding. Each Phrasing Fun activity was designed for one-on-one guided instruction, small groups, or whole-class instruction on the overhead projector. By following the Fantastic Five Format, the student is assured success in meaningful phrasing practice to develop fluency and comprehension.

Strategies: phrased reading; repeated oral reading; active listening; reading high-frequency, content, and sight words

Materials
- no additional materials are required

Directions

1. Copy a class set or group set of each pair of Phrasing Fun stories.

2. Give each student a copy of the first page of the pair of reproducibles for the story you have chosen.

3. Read the text following the Fantastic Five Format (described on page 8).
  Step 1: Modeled Fluency—Model how to read each phrase.
  Step 2: Echo Reading—Read one phrase at a time as students repeat.
  Step 3: Choral Reading—Guide students as they read with phrasing along with you.
  Step 4: Independent Fluency—Have students read the phrases to you.
  Step 5: Reverse Echo Reading—Have students read the phrases, and then repeat their phrasing, expression, and fluency.

4. Give each student a copy of the second page of the reproducible for the story you have chosen. (It has the same phrases as reproducible 1, but it is written in an ongoing text format and has at least two additional paragraphs of related text. This reproducible gives students the opportunity to transfer their fluently read phrases to a paragraph format.)

5. Choral read the reproducible together. Then, invite the group to read it aloud to you.

6. Repeat this activity with additional reading selections for further practice.

7. Invite students to practice their phrasing and fluency by reading a familiar book.

Extension

Copy a page from a class textbook. Have students use a pencil to draw slash marks to break apart the first paragraph into phrases (as in the first page of each set of reproducibles). Provide time for them to practice the Fantastic Five Format prior to reading the paragraph, and then have them continue through the rest of the page.

Visiting the Aquarium

Kyra and Kevin

woke up early

on Saturday morning.

They knew that

the aquarium was open

from 9 A.M. to 6 P.M.

They wanted

to get there in time

to see the shark feeding.

That is when

the scuba diver

enters the shark tank!

Phrasing Fun

Visiting the Aquarium

Kyra and Kevin woke up early on Saturday morning. They knew that the aquarium was open from 9 A.M. to 6 P.M. They wanted to get there in time to see the shark feeding. That is when the scuba diver enters the shark tank!

Kyra and Kevin were among the first visitors to the aquarium. They purchased tickets and hurried to the shark tank. The scuba diver stood by the side of the tank. He adjusted his scuba mask and sat on the side of the tank. First, he pushed backward to enter the water. Kyra and Kevin could see him do a slow somersault underwater. Then, he straightened out and kicked back to the surface. A helper handed him a large bucket.

The sharks seemed to know him. They began swimming closer in smaller circles. He dived down and began scattering bits of fish from the bucket. The sharks dashed about, scooping up the pieces of meat. By the time the bucket was empty, the sharks swam more slowly and took longer to go after the meat. Other fish ate the leftover bits that floated to the bottom.

Developing Reading Fluency • Gr. 5 © 2004 Creative Teaching Press

Peach Baskets and Balls

How do you think peaches

are part of basketball's beginning?

No, they were not

the first things thrown

through a hoop!

Two peach baskets

and a soccer ball

were used

in the first basketball game.

Phrasing Fun

Peach Baskets and Balls

How do you think peaches are part of basketball's beginning? No, they were not the first things thrown through a hoop! Two peach baskets and a soccer ball were used in the first basketball game.

Dr. James Naismith was a teacher in Massachusetts. He had a particularly rowdy group of students one winter. The head of the school asked Dr. Naismith to invent a game that would keep the boys out of trouble and in good health. It was a very cold winter, so the boys had to play inside. Dr. Naismith tried a variety of games, but none appealed to the boys until his game with raised baskets. He put one peach basket on each end of the gym. He created rules and used a soccer ball to demonstrate.

Since a peach basket has a woven bottom, the soccer ball would stay in the basket after it was placed there. Students had to use a stepladder to get the ball from the basket each time someone scored. Still, it was worth the trouble! The game required skill and teamwork, and the game was a hit.

Developing Reading Fluency • Gr. 5 © 2004 Creative Teaching Press

How to Become an Olympic Athlete

Do you enjoy watching

the Olympic Games?

It may seem

when you watch the athletes

on television

that they live in a different world

from yours.

Actually,

athletes come from

all kinds of backgrounds

and parts of the world.

They share

a deep love of sport.

Developing Reading Fluency • Gr. 5 © 2004 Creative Teaching Press

Phrasing Fun

How to Become an Olympic Athlete

Do you enjoy watching the Olympic Games? It may seem when you watch the athletes on television that they live in a different world from yours. Actually, athletes come from all kinds of backgrounds and parts of the world. They share a deep love of sport. Could you be an Olympic athlete? Sure! It requires hard work, but the steps are similar for each sport.

First, you need to choose a sport you like. Hard work and lots of practice are more important than your beginning talent. If you do not like the sport, it is hard to motivate yourself to do the work it takes to be one of the best in that sport.

Next, you need to find a place to practice. You will want to find a dedicated coach and other people who also enjoy the sport. Even if your sport is a solitary one like archery, it helps to have others around to learn from.

Eventually, you'll start competing, find a sponsor, and participate in your sport's national championships. It will take time, but if you persevere and follow these simple steps, it could one day be you standing on an Olympic podium!

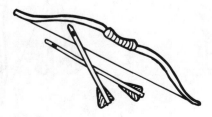

Developing Reading Fluency • Gr. 5 © 2004 Creative Teaching Press

American Soccer and Football

Teams have kicked

round balls around

since ancient Rome.

In the early 1800s,

British parents invented a game

where a ball was kicked

into a goal.

They used it

to teach children teamwork.

Teams agreed on rules

and called the game football.

Phrasing Fun

American Soccer and Football

Teams have kicked round balls around since ancient Rome. In the early 1800s, British parents invented a game where a ball was kicked into a goal. They used it to teach children teamwork. Teams agreed on rules and called the game football. (Americans refer to the sport as soccer. We will explain that later.)

The game became popular on American college campuses. Time passed. Football rules changed in America. More players were added. They began to allow the use of hands. The game began to look less like modern soccer and more like modern football. The name did not change, but the game did. This is why American football and European football are very different games.

Eventually, European football made a return to America. But football in America meant fifteen players, the use of hands, touchdowns, and other rules that no one else used. So Americans gave the sport of kicking a round ball into the other team's goal the name of soccer.

Developing Reading Fluency • Gr. 5 © 2004 Creative Teaching Press

Asian Kites

The way that a mobile

moves and balances

is part of its art.

In the same way,

an Asian kite is judged

by how it moves

and by the way it looks.

It must fly well

and look beautiful.

Phrasing Fun

Asian Kites

The way that a mobile moves and balances is part of its art. In the same way, an Asian kite is judged by how it moves and by the way it looks. It must fly well and look beautiful.

Asian kites are made from bamboo frames, a special, tough paper, paint, and kite string. Asian kites may be as large as a room and as heavy as a young elephant. They may be as small as your thumbnail. A typical kite is between 4 and 15 square feet. Compare this to an American kite, which is more commonly around 3 square feet or less. Another difference between American and Asian kites is that all Asian kites are made by artists. In America, handmade kites are not very common.

Asian kites may also be different in purpose. While American kites are flown mostly as a way to relax, Asian kites may actually be designed to do battle! At many kite festivals, fighting kites compete to break each other's strings. Bits of cut glass and porcelain glued to the kite strings help them cut the string of another kite. A losing kite is chased and the first person to find the fallen kite gets to keep it.

Developing Reading Fluency • Gr. 5 © 2004 Creative Teaching Press

Homes

Homes vary

from culture to culture.

In America,

we live in homes

and apartment buildings.

In some cultures,

people still live in tents.

In other areas,

many families may live together

in one house.

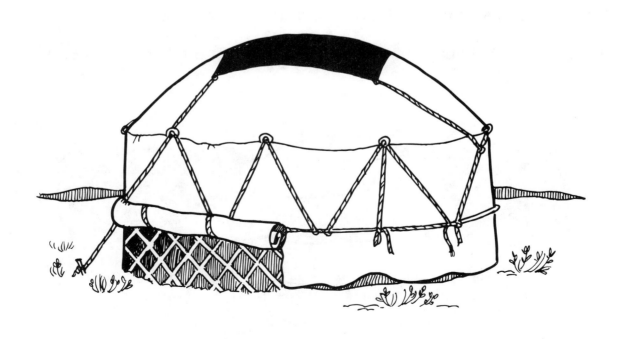

Developing Reading Fluency • Gr. 5 © 2004 Creative Teaching Press

Phrasing Fun

Homes

Homes vary from culture to culture. In America, we live in homes and apartment buildings. In some cultures, people still live in tents. In other areas, many families may live together in one house.

What determines the kind of dwelling people live in? People make homes that fit the way they live. Can people who follow animal herds live in large brick houses? They cannot do so very easily. Large brick houses are better suited to a group of people who do not move often.

People also build houses that fit their environment. Would it be wise to build a house from ice and snow in the middle of Texas? Such a house would not last long on a warm Texas day. However, an igloo is a great way for a person in the Arctic to shelter his family. The materials are easily found, and the insulating snow keeps everyone inside warm. Because the materials do not cost anything, they can leave the igloo when they follow animal herds.

Students who are not chunking groups of words in phrases end up with poorer comprehension since they are overly focusing on the print rather than the message hidden within. This explicit strategy is best for students who don't seem to understand the concept of chunking words. When most people speak, they phrase a whole sentence or thought as one phrase. Students have a hard time hearing the phrases, so telling them to "read like talking" doesn't always work. Some students simply require more explicit instruction. The activities in this section are designed for individuals, small groups, or even the whole class. They will provide the visual cues for those students struggling with understanding what a "phrase" really is.

Strategies: phrased reading; visual cues; apply and transfer; scaffolding phrase size

Materials
- no additional materials are required

Directions

1. Decide which students need practice with phrased text activities by using the assessments at the beginning of this book. Students who still read word-by-word or only two- to three-word phrases should participate.

2. Photocopy a set of phrased text reproducibles for each student.

3. Give each student a copy of the first page that contains the visual cue: ◆
   Explain that he or she will train his or her eyes to look at chunks of words at a time. (Due to the explicit nature of the instruction, the student's mind will be focused on grouping words instead of on meaning. Therefore, rereading a few times for comprehension will be important.)

4. Read the first few sentences following the Fantastic Five Format (described on page 8).
   Step 1: Modeled Fluency—Model how to read each phrase.
   Step 2: Echo Reading—Read one phrase at a time as students repeat.
   Step 3: Choral Reading—Guide students as they read with phrasing along with you.
   Step 4: Independent Fluency—Have students read the phrases to you.
   Step 5: Reverse Echo Reading—Have students read the phrases, and then repeat their phrasing, expression, and fluency.

5. Have the student or group continue with the rest on its own.

6. Immediately read the page without visual cues together using the choral reading technique.

7. Finally, have students individually read the page without visual cues.

Extension

Invite students to preview the next section of a textbook or reading anthology you are using in class. Have them rewrite the paragraphs showing visual cues. Then, have them practice reading the phrased text before reading their textbook.

The Ancient Aztec People

Mexico was once home ✦ to the Aztec people. ✦ They wore bright clothes ✦ made of woven cloth, ✦ feathers, ✦ and jaguar skins. ✦ They made beautiful fans and jewelry. ✦ They carved ✦ huge sculptures and reliefs ✦ from wood and stone. ✦ They wrote poems, ✦ songs, ✦ and stories. ✦ They were brilliant farmers ✦ who figured out ✦ how to irrigate their crops ✦ by bringing water ✦ up the mountain. ✦ They were fierce warriors. ✦

What did Aztec children do? ✦ They lived with their families ✦ when they were very young. ✦ Aztec children ate beans and corn. ✦ They ate lizards and insect eggs. ✦ They used cacao beans ✦ to make chocolate. ✦ When they were old enough, ✦ they went to school. ✦

Children of farmers ✦ went to one school. ✦ Children of rulers ✦ went to another school. ✦ Children of rulers ✦ lived at the school. ✦ Children of farmers ✦ could go home at night. ✦

Aztec students learned to read, ✦ write, ✦ and do math. ✦ They worked hard in school. ✦ They kept fires burning all night ✦ for the Aztec priests ✦ and kept public places ✦ in the villages and cities clean. ✦ They also learned to make art. ✦

Art was important to the Aztecs. ✦ Today, ✦ many artists study Aztec art. ✦ They copy Aztec patterns. ✦ Artists love the Aztec colors and lines. ✦ Sometimes they use Aztec ideas in new ways. ✦ One rock carving is an Aztec calendar. ✦ It is beautiful. ✦ It is called the Sun Stone. ✦ It told the Aztecs ✦ what to do on each day. ✦ It also told their story ✦ of the world. ✦ What kind of stories ✦ does art tell today?

Developing Reading Fluency • Gr. 5 © 2004 Creative Teaching Press

The Ancient Aztec People

Mexico was once home to the Aztec people. They wore bright clothes made of woven cloth, feathers, and jaguar skins. They made beautiful fans and jewelry. They carved huge sculptures and reliefs from wood and stone. They wrote poems, songs, and stories. They were brilliant farmers who figured out how to irrigate their crops by bringing water up the mountain. They were fierce warriors.

What did Aztec children do? They lived with their families when they were very young. Aztec children ate beans and corn. They ate lizards and insect eggs. They used cacao beans to make chocolate. When they were old enough, they went to school.

Children of farmers went to one school. Children of rulers went to another school. Children of rulers lived at the school. Children of farmers could go home at night.

Aztec students learned to read, write, and do math. They worked hard in school. They kept fires burning all night for the Aztec priests and kept public places in the villages and cities clean. They also learned to make art.

Art was important to the Aztecs. Today, many artists study Aztec art. They copy Aztec patterns. Artists love the Aztec colors and lines. Sometimes they use Aztec ideas in new ways. One rock carving is an Aztec calendar. It is beautiful. It is called the Sun Stone. It told the Aztecs what to do on each day. It also told their story of the world. What kind of stories does art tell today?

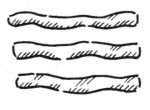

Phrased Text

Jazz Music

Jazz music is American music. ✦ It has its roots ✦ in American spirituals. ✦ Jazz music tells about life ✦ in America. ✦ Many famous jazz players ✦ were born in America, ✦ but people like jazz ✦ all over the world. ✦

Jazz music is a kind of art. ✦ It tells in a song ✦ or piece of music ✦ how the artist feels. ✦ Jazz music can sound happy, ✦ sad, ✦ or even silly. ✦

Some artists ✦ like to show jazz players ✦ in their work. ✦ The artist chooses colors ✦ that show the mood ✦ of the music. ✦ What color would you choose ✦ to show happy music? ✦ What color would you choose ✦ to show sad music? ✦

Lionel Milton is a painter. ✦ He paints scenes of jazz players ✦ in bright colors. ✦ Some of his paintings are huge! ✦ They fill a city wall ✦ with a scene from jazz music! ✦ Milton loves jazz. ✦ His paintings show how he feels ✦ when he listens to jazz. ✦

Herman Leonard ✦ is a photographer. ✦ He took pictures ✦ of men and women ✦ playing and singing jazz. ✦ His pictures of jazz musicians ✦ show the history of jazz in America. ✦

You can dance and paint ✦ to jazz music. ✦ Listen to jazz music. ✦ Try to hear the story ✦ the sound tells. ✦ How does it make you feel?

Developing Reading Fluency • Gr. 5 © 2004 Creative Teaching Press

Jazz Music

Jazz music is American music. It has its roots in American spirituals. Jazz music tells about life in America. Many famous jazz players were born in America, but people like jazz all over the world.

Jazz music is a kind of art. It tells in a song or piece of music how the artist feels. Jazz music can sound happy, sad, or even silly.

Some artists like to show jazz players in their work. The artist chooses colors that show the mood of the music. What color would you choose to show happy music? What color would you choose to show sad music?

Lionel Milton is a painter. He paints scenes of jazz players in bright colors. Some of his paintings are huge! They fill a city wall with a scene from jazz music! Milton loves jazz. His paintings show how he feels when he listens to jazz.

Herman Leonard is a photographer. He took pictures of men and women playing and singing jazz. His pictures of jazz musicians show the history of jazz in America.

You can dance and paint to jazz music. Listen to jazz music. Try to hear the story the sound tells. How does it make you feel?

Developing Reading Fluency • Gr. 5 © 2004 Creative Teaching Press

Phrased Text

Auguste Renoir

Auguste Renoir was a painter. ✦ He was an impressionist painter ✦ who helped change ✦ the way the French ✦ thought about art. ✦ He enjoyed painting with bright colors. ✦ He often painted outdoors ✦ so that he could take advantage ✦ of natural light. ✦ He was older ✦ when he began to sell ✦ enough of his paintings ✦ to live comfortably. ✦ It was around this time ✦ that he married. ✦

He had three sons. ✦ He liked being a father ✦ and he had very strong convictions ✦ about raising children. ✦ He said that children ✦ should see bright colors ✦ and have simple toys. ✦ He thought children ✦ should explore ✦ while they were young, ✦ and he did not provide his sons ✦ with any formal schooling ✦ until they were ten years old. ✦ He believed that ✦ they would catch up quickly ✦ when they were finally ✦ given school lessons. ✦

Renoir liked to paint pictures of his boys. ✦ He did not ✦ make the boys sit still. ✦ He waited until they were quiet. ✦ He painted ✦ when they ate, ✦ drew pictures, ✦ read books, ✦ and played with blocks. ✦ In a similar fashion, ✦ he painted some of the neighbors, ✦ his children's friends, ✦ and some of his wife's relatives ✦ who lived and worked for them. ✦

Renoir liked to have his friends visit. ✦ Grown-ups and children ✦ would come to his house. ✦ They talked and laughed. ✦ Renoir's wife, ✦ Aline, ✦ enjoyed cooking and caring ✦ for her children. ✦She hosted their friends, ✦ and they often enjoyed the company ✦ of other artists. ✦ They watched Renoir paint ✦ during the day. ✦ Renoir often painted his friends ✦ when they visited. ✦ The paintings tell about ✦ the happiness in his house.

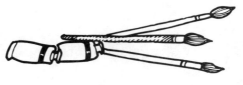

Developing Reading Fluency • Gr. 5 © 2004 Creative Teaching Press

Auguste Renoir

Auguste Renoir was a painter. He was an impressionist painter who helped change the way the French thought about art. He enjoyed painting with bright colors. He often painted outdoors so that he could take advantage of natural light. He was older when he began to sell enough of his paintings to live comfortably. It was around this time that he married.

He had three sons. He liked being a father and he had very strong convictions about raising children. He said that children should see bright colors and have simple toys. He thought children should explore while they were young, and he did not provide his sons with any formal schooling until they were ten years old. He believed that they would catch up quickly when they were finally given school lessons.

Renoir liked to paint pictures of his boys. He did not make the boys sit still. He waited until they were quiet. He painted when they ate, drew pictures, read books, and played with blocks. In a similar fashion, he painted some of the neighbors, his children's friends, and some of his wife's relatives who lived and worked for them.

Renoir liked to have his friends visit. Grown-ups and children would come to his house. They talked and laughed. Renoir's wife, Aline, enjoyed cooking and caring for her children. She hosted their friends, and they often enjoyed the company of other artists. They watched Renoir paint during the day. Renoir often painted his friends when they visited. The paintings tell about the happiness in his house.

Developing Reading Fluency • Gr. 5 © 2004 Creative Teaching Press

 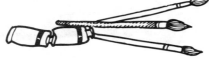

Phrased Text

F.A.I.N.—Fund-raising for Animals in Need

Have you ever visited ✦ an animal shelter? ✦ Perhaps you know someone ✦ who has adopted a pet ✦ from an animal shelter. ✦ The animal shelters are homes ✦ to animals in need of ✦ loving families. ✦ Many animal shelters ✦ depend on donations from animal lovers ✦ to provide services. ✦ Ashley and Micaela ✦ are young animal lovers ✦ who are dedicated to helping animals in need. ✦

Ashley and Micaela met at school. ✦ They were both animal lovers. ✦ They decided to form a non-profit organization ✦ called F.A.I.N. ✦ Their goal would be to plan and hold ✦ various fund-raisers to earn money ✦ for the local animal shelter. ✦ Every spare minute of their time ✦ was spent thinking ✦ of products or services to offer, ✦ when events would take place, ✦ what supplies would be needed, ✦ and estimating ✦ how much money they could earn. ✦ They would give every penny ✦ to the animal shelter. ✦ Their mission was a success! ✦

What is even more amazing ✦ is that these two animal lovers ✦ were only in the fifth grade! ✦ In fact, ✦ in a period of only two months, ✦ Micaela and Ashley collected ✦ 50 blankets for the shelter ✦ and donated $300.00 collected from a bake sale! ✦ Now that's dedication! ✦

Their non-profit organization ✦ is still going strong. ✦ Every year, ✦ they find more and more supporters ✦ who join them in helping animals in need. ✦ Perhaps you would like to follow in their footsteps. ✦ What organization would you create? ✦ What would your goals be? ✦ Whom would you like to help?

Developing Reading Fluency • Gr. 5 © 2004 Creative Teaching Press

F.A.I.N.—Fund-raising for Animals in Need

Have you ever visited an animal shelter? Perhaps you know someone who has adopted a pet from an animal shelter. The animal shelters are homes to animals in need of loving families. Many animal shelters depend on donations from animal lovers to provide services. Ashley and Micaela are young animal lovers who are dedicated to helping animals in need.

Ashley and Micaela met at school. They were both animal lovers. They decided to form a non-profit organization called F.A.I.N. Their goal would be to plan and hold various fund-raisers to earn money for the local animal shelter. Every spare minute of their time was spent thinking of products or services to offer, when events would take place, what supplies would be needed, and estimating how much money they could earn. They would give every penny to the animal shelter. Their mission was a success!

What is even more amazing is that these two animal lovers were only in the fifth grade! In fact, in a period of only two months, Micaela and Ashley collected 50 blankets for the shelter and donated $300.00 collected from a bake sale! Now that's dedication!

Their non-profit organization is still going strong. Every year, they find more and more supporters who join them in helping animals in need. Perhaps you would like to follow in their footsteps. What organization would you create? What would your goals be? Whom would you like to help?

Phrased Text

Chocolate Chip Cookies

Who doesn't love ✦ a warm, gooey chocolate chip cookie? ✦ Whether they're fresh from the oven ✦ or purchased from your local grocery store, ✦ chocolate chip cookies ✦ have warmed people from the inside out ✦ since 1930. ✦ If you enjoy chocolate chip cookies, ✦ then you owe your thanks to Ruth Wakefield. ✦

Ruth Wakefield worked as a dietitian ✦ and lectured on food. ✦ In 1930, ✦ she and her husband, Kenneth, ✦ purchased a toll house ✦ in Massachusetts. ✦ Originally built in 1709, ✦ its purpose was to give tired travelers ✦ the ability to change their horses ✦ and eat home-cooked meals ✦ in exchange for a toll (fee). ✦ More than 200 years later, ✦ the Wakefields opened the Toll House Inn. ✦ It was a simple version of a modern motel. ✦ Ruth enjoyed making delicious meals ✦ and tasty desserts for her guests. ✦

One day, ✦ while making butter cookies, ✦ she decided to add pieces of a Nestlé chocolate bar. ✦ She was surprised to find ✦ how delicious these new cookies tasted! ✦ She began serving them ✦ to her guests. ✦ The cookies were so popular ✦ that her recipe was soon published ✦ in a Boston newspaper! ✦ Of course, ✦ this boosted the sales of the chocolate bar ✦ created by Daniel Peter and Henri Nestlé ✦ at the same time. ✦ They began to work together. ✦ Ruth Wakefield gave Nestlé her recipe ✦ in exchange for a lifetime supply of chocolate. ✦

Today, making these cookies is easier. ✦ Instead of having to break a bar into bits, ✦ you can add a package of chocolate chips ✦ to your favorite cookie recipe. ✦ The popularity of the chocolate chip cookie ✦ continues today.

Developing Reading Fluency • Gr. 5 © 2004 Creative Teaching Press

Chocolate Chip Cookies

Who doesn't love a warm, gooey chocolate chip cookie? Whether they're fresh from the oven or purchased from your local grocery store, chocolate chip cookies have warmed people from the inside out since 1930. If you enjoy chocolate chip cookies, then you owe your thanks to Ruth Wakefield.

Ruth Wakefield worked as a dietitian and lectured on food. In 1930, she and her husband, Kenneth, purchased a toll house in Massachusetts. Originally built in 1709, its purpose was to give tired travelers the ability to change their horses and eat home-cooked meals in exchange for a toll (fee). More than 200 years later, the Wakefields opened the Toll House Inn. It was a simple version of a modern motel. Ruth enjoyed making delicious meals and tasty desserts for her guests.

One day, while making butter cookies, she decided to add pieces of a Nestle chocolaté bar. She was surprised to find how delicious these new cookies tasted! She began serving them to her guests. The cookies were so popular that her recipe was soon published in a Boston newspaper! Of course, this boosted the sales of the chocolate bar created by Daniel Peter and Henri Nestlé at the same time. They began to work together. Ruth Wakefield gave Nestlé her recipe in exchange for a lifetime supply of chocolate.

Today, making these cookies is easier. Instead of having to break a bar into bits, you can add a package of chocolate chips to your favorite cookie recipe. The popularity of the chocolate chip cookie continues today.

Developing Reading Fluency • Gr. 5 © 2004 Creative Teaching Press

Phrased Text

Funny Uses for Common Things!

You will never believe ✦ some of the unusual uses ✦ for household items ✦ you use almost every day! ✦ Let us take a look ✦ at two common items ✦ you probably have in your home ✦ that could be used ✦ in different ways. ✦ Some uses may sound a bit silly, ✦ but they are all true! ✦

First, ✦ let's think about ✦ the ever popular sandwich spread—✦ peanut butter! ✦ Sure, ✦ you know it tastes great ✦ on celery, on crackers, or mixed with jelly, ✦ but what other things can it do? ✦ You can use peanut butter ✦ to remove bubble gum ✦ from your hair! ✦ If mice are a problem ✦ in your house, ✦ you can catch them better ✦ with peanut butter than with cheese! ✦ The next time you eat peanut butter, ✦ these two funny facts ✦ should put a smile ✦ on your face. ✦

Now let's consider the chalk ✦ you may have ✦ at school or home. ✦ Did you know ✦ that you can prevent ✦ an ant invasion ✦ using your chalk? ✦ It's true! ✦ Ants will not cross a chalk line, ✦ so the next time ✦ you have an ant problem at home, ✦ simply draw a line of chalk ✦ around windows, doors, and water pipes. ✦ That will send a simple message ✦ for them to stay away. ✦ Perhaps you've tried ✦ using a screwdriver, ✦ but it kept slipping. ✦ Once again, ✦ your chalk comes in handy! ✦ If you rub chalk ✦ on the tip of your screwdriver, ✦ then it will not slip anymore. ✦ So, ✦ when you decide to throw away ✦ that piece of chalk, ✦ perhaps you'll save it ✦ for one of these purposes.

There are so many other ✦ interesting uses ✦ for common things, ✦ but some of them ✦ should be left to future discovery!

Developing Reading Fluency • Gr. 5 © 2004 Creative Teaching Press

Funny Uses for Common Things!

You will never believe some of the unusual uses for household items you use almost every day! Let us take a look at two common items you probably have in your home that could be used in different ways. Some uses may sound a bit silly, but they are all true!

First, let's think about the ever popular sandwich spread—peanut butter! Sure, you know it tastes great on celery, on crackers, or mixed with jelly, but what other things can it do? You can use peanut butter to remove bubble gum from your hair! If mice are a problem in your house, you can catch them better with peanut butter than with cheese! The next time you eat peanut butter, these two funny facts should put a smile on your face.

Now let's consider the chalk you may have at school or home. Did you know that you can prevent an ant invasion using your chalk? It's true! Ants will not cross a chalk line, so the next time you have an ant problem at home, simply draw a line of chalk around windows, doors, and water pipes. That will send a simple message for them to stay away. Perhaps you've tried using a screwdriver, but it kept slipping. Once again, your chalk comes in handy! If you rub chalk on the tip of your screwdriver, then it will not slip anymore. So, when you decide to throw away that piece of chalk, perhaps you'll save it for one of these purposes.

There are so many other interesting uses for common things, but some of them should be left for future discovery!

Phrased Text

Reader's Theater

Reader's Theater is a motivating and exciting way for students to mature into fluent and expressive readers. Reader's Theater does not use any props, costumes, or materials other than the script, which allows the focus to stay on fluent and expressive reading. The "actors" must tell the story using only their voices and rely on their tone of voice, expression, phrasing, and fluency to express the story to the audience. Students are reading for a purpose, which highly motivates them because they take on the roles of characters and bring the characters to life through voice inflection. Each Reader's Theater script is designed for a group of four students. However, the scripts can be modified, if necessary. For example, students can double-up on roles to incorporate paired reading.

Strategies: repeated oral reading for groups of four; choral reading; paired reading

Materials
- highlighters
- colored file folders

Directions

1. Make four copies of each play. (Each play is several pages long.) Staple the pages together along the left side of the script (not the top). Highlight a different character's part on each script.

2. Gather four folders of the same color for each play. Put one copy of the script in each folder. Write the title of the play and the name of the highlighted character (e.g., Troy, Denise) on the front of each folder.

3. Divide the class into groups of four. Give each student in a group the same color folder (containing the same script).

4. Have students first read the entire script. (Research supports having students read all of the roles for the first day or two to fully comprehend the story.) Then, have each student choose which part he or she will perform, or assign each student a part. Have students switch folders so that each student has the script with the highlighted character's part that he or she will play.

5. Invite students to perform their play for the whole class, another group, a buddy class, or their parents.

Extension

Invite students to write a Reader's Theater script to be used with four readers. Type the script, and follow the five steps above using the script created by the students.

The Chili Cook-off

Characters: Troy   Tom
              Denise   Narrator

Narrator

The annual Tri-City Chili Cook-off is tomorrow! For the past eight years, Troy, Denise, and Tom have participated. Secretly, they've always hoped to make better chili than the other contestants. Today, they are getting ready to make their best chili ever!

Troy

Let's get started! All of the basic ingredients are ready. We just need our Secret Spice Mix. Tom, will you please get me the crushed red peppers and garlic pepper from the cupboard?

Tom

Sure! I brought my special meat recipe. We're sure to win first prize this year! We came so close last year, but I have to admit that the Olsons did make better chili. This time I changed my meat recipe a bit. I've been working on it for three weeks!

Denise

I made a few changes in cooking my beans as well. They should be even better than last year.

Troy

With all of these improvements and my Secret Spice Mix we just have to win this year! First, we need to chop the fresh onions. Who will do that?

Tom

I've already got it under control! They are washed and ready to be chopped. I'll chop the garlic cloves, too. I can't wait for the judges to taste our chili!

Troy

It'll knock their socks off!

Developing Reading Fluency • Gr. 5 © 2004 Creative Teaching Press

Reader's Theater

The Chili Cook-off

Denise

Burn them off is more like it! How much chili powder do you think we should use in our sauce this year?

Troy

I think that three tablespoons should be enough for each batch we make.

Narrator

Each friend gets busy with his or her part of the chili-making process. Denise is getting the tomato sauce ready for the hot sauce they add. It gives the chili a good kick! Troy is busy making his Secret Spice Mix using red pepper flakes, chili powder, cumin, paprika, cocoa, and sugar. Tom is busy browning the meat on the stove.

Denise

What did the Olsons win last year as first prize?

Tom

They won a trip to Paris, France, a new chili pot, and a blue ribbon! This year the prize is $2,500.00!

Narrator

They all started talking about what they could do with their portion of the winnings. They were sure they were going to win first prize!

Tom

Wait a minute! We shouldn't count our chickens before they hatch! How do we know if we'll get the money at all? Maybe we'll come in second again.

Troy

I could settle for that. The second prize is $500.00.

Denise

Let's just focus on trying our best. Any way you look at it, we'll be making some dynamite chili! It already smells so good in here! Tom, how's your meat coming along?

Developing Reading Fluency • Gr. 5 © 2004 Creative Teaching Press

The Chili Cook-off

Tom

It's almost ready for the onions and garlic. Are your beans ready?

Denise

In just a few minutes. Troy, how is your Secret Spice Mix coming along?

Troy

Done! Let's get cooking! This is sure to be the hottest chili at the cook-off!

Narrator

Each friend finished with his or her part of the chili recipe.

Troy

All set? Let's mix it all together! Here we go!

Narrator

They mixed the chili, added the Secret Spice Mix, and put it all in the slow cooker to simmer. They wanted all of the juices to mix with the spices.

Denise

Now for the corn bread! We can't serve chili without corn bread!

Narrator

While Denise made the corn bread, the boys discussed what drinks they wanted to have handy.

Denise

Done! We're ready for the big day! It's time to rest. Who wants to watch a movie?

Tom and Troy

I do!

Narrator

They all met at Troy's house the next morning. They got their chili, the corn bread, the drinks, bowls, spoons, and napkins. Then, they were off to the Tri-City Chili Cook-off!

The Chili Cook-off

Tom

That's our spot right there! We're number 16. The table is already set up for us. We just need to plug in our slow cooker, set up our food, and wait for the judges. Let's do it!

Narrator

After setting up their booths, the contestants usually greet one another and try the other competitors' chili. Troy, Tom, and Denise walked around and sampled some of the chili that they were hoping to beat.

Troy

Wow! Did you try the chili at booth 27? It was amazing! They're going to be hard to beat!

Tom

I liked the spices in the chili I tasted at booth 35. Did you try that one?

Troy

I didn't make it that far. I ran into my friends Erin and Fred. They're in booth 22. They had chili that reminded me of ours last year.

Denise

I still think we have a good chance of winning, but I'll be the first to admit that the competition is tough. Everyone takes this so seriously! I thought it was just supposed to be fun.

Troy

It is, but it's fun to win, too!

Denise

Here come the judges! Quick! Get them each a bowl and napkin before they get here!

Narrator

The judges tasted their chili. They said it was tasty and spicy, but the three friends could tell that everyone participating got the same reaction. They would just have to wait for the results.

Developing Reading Fluency • Gr. 5 © 2004 Creative Teaching Press

The Chili Cook-off

Denise
Well, we made the best chili we knew how! Now, we'll just have to wait and see what happens.

Tom
Let's go visit with the other contestants and try some more chili!

Troy
I'm with you!

Narrator
An hour later, the announcement came over the loudspeaker that the judges had made their decision. All contestants were invited to meet at the head table for the announcement of the winners.

All
Let's go!

Narrator
The judge announced the third-prize winner. Booth number 22 won a new slow cooker and 20 cans of chili!

Denise
They did have a great recipe! The judges made a good choice on that one.

Narrator
The judges announced that they had a tie for second place. They awarded the $500.00 to be split between the chefs at booths 35 and 27.

Troy
I knew booth 27 would win! That was my favorite! Well, not counting our own.

Narrator
The judge said, "And now . . . for the first prize. The first-prize winners today will be receiving the blue ribbon, $2,500.00, and the chance to have their prize-winning recipe published on the first page of our annual cookbook! The winner is . . . ."
(left open-ended for predictions)

Developing Reading Fluency • Gr. 5 © 2004 Creative Teaching Press

Reader's Theater

Voyage to the Bottom of the Sea

Characters: Brenton   Trenton
                 Danielle   Dr. Linda

Dr. Linda
Welcome aboard! You must be the three people who had the highest bid in my auction! You're our first twins to go on this adventure! Are you ready for the adventure of your life?

Brenton and Trenton
You bet!

Dr. Linda
Actually, it's so much smaller than a submarine that we call it a submersible. It goes underwater like a submarine, but is easier to control and maneuver. Follow me and I'll take you to *Shiloh*. **Shiloh** stands for **S**ubmersible **H**umans **I**nvestigating **L**ower **O**cean **H**abitats.

Trenton
Wow! I never knew that! I thought you named it after the dog in that book I read in school!

Danielle
Is this your first submersible that can take people on underwater adventures?

Dr. Linda
This is actually our fifth submersible. The other four take two scientists and one guest at a time. *Shiloh* is the first submersible to carry up to six passengers down to the ocean's floor.

Brenton
How often do you take people like us on undersea adventures?

Dr. Linda
It's very rare. We've only done it once before. Normally, we take our families, other scientists, and college students who are studying oceanography.

Developing Reading Fluency • Gr. 5 © 2004 Creative Teaching Press

Voyage to the Bottom of the Sea

Danielle

Why did you put this adventure on an online auction giving anyone the chance to go?

Dr. Linda

To be honest with you, we are having a hard time getting enough money to continue our underwater research laboratory. It was getting more expensive than we had expected, so we decided to try this approach.

Trenton

Do you think the amount we each paid with the highest bids will be enough money to help you continue your research?

Dr. Linda

It's a good start. It was a bit of an experiment to see what type of interest would be out there and how much people would be willing to pay.

Brenton

That reminds me of the time when that pop star was willing to pay millions of dollars to fly in a space shuttle. Did he ever get to do that?

Dr. Linda

For safety reasons, he still hasn't had that opportunity. Don't worry! *Shiloh* is much safer. By the way, you don't have any problems in tight spaces do you?

Danielle

No way! I'm all set. I even took scuba diving lessons last summer! I can't wait to see the fish and other ocean creatures.

Trenton

How long will be we able to investigate?

Dr. Linda

We'll be down there for about an hour. We are packed in so tightly that it gets uncomfortable if you aren't used to it. That's enough time for you to enjoy the mysteries of the deep.

Developing Reading Fluency • Gr. 5 © 2004 Creative Teaching Press

Voyage to the Bottom of the Sea

Danielle

I just can't wait!

Trenton

Is it true that you only go down in a submersible once every few weeks?

Dr. Linda

Yes, we usually investigate the depths of the ocean using our ROV's. That stands for remotely operated vehicles.

Brenton

Oh! I know all about those! I read about those at school. They can explore farther, faster, and more safely than what we are going on.

Trenton

That's right! I remember now. Mr. Dominic taught us about that last year! The ROV's can carry more equipment. Is that right, Dr. Linda?

Dr. Linda

You have a good memory! It's true. The ROV's are attached by a cable to the ship I am usually on. My ROV's can carry lights, cameras, and sometimes sonar that . . .

Danielle
(interrupting)
I know what sonar is! Sonar uses sound waves to find objects underwater. Isn't that how some sea mammals find their way around in the dark water?

Dr. Linda

You're right. Anyway, the ROV's are easier to use and can stay underwater for longer periods of time. Well, it looks like we've almost reached our destination!

Brenton

Look! It's a pirate ship!

Danielle

No way! Is that really a pirate ship? It can't be!

Developing Reading Fluency • Gr. 5 © 2004 Creative Teaching Press

Voyage to the Bottom of the Sea

Dr. Linda
It's not a pirate ship, but it is a sunken ship. Surprise! This is what we will be investigating today! We need to collect data about this ship so we can try to identify where it came from, how long it's been here, and other clues about its past.

Trenton and Brenton
Wow!

Danielle
Unbelievable!

Dr. Linda
Believe it! What you see in front of you is a ship that we believe sank to the bottom of the ocean during World War II. It's like a museum inside since it holds secrets and important information about that era.

Danielle
Can we go all the way around it?

Dr. Linda
We can do better than that. We can go in it! On the other side of this ship, there is a huge hole. We can get very close and then send in the camera that we guide with these controls right here.

Trenton
It's like a robot! Can we see what the camera sees?

Brenton
Look! On the TV! It's a shark! No, it's a whale! No, it's an eel! What is that thing anyway?

Dr. Linda
That's a giant squid! I know it's hard to see due to the darkness, but if you look just beyond the light from *Shiloh,* you'll see a few of the most mysterious sea creatures you could ever imagine!

Developing Reading Fluency • Gr. 5 © 2004 Creative Teaching Press

Voyage to the Bottom of the Sea

Danielle
What's that light over there?

Dr. Linda
That's one of the bioluminescent fish that glow underwater. Isn't it beautiful? Okay. Let's follow the eye of the camera. Can you tell which part of the ship it is searching right now?

Trenton
It almost looks like a bedroom. Are those bunk beds? There are so many of them stacked in that tiny room! How could anyone live like that?

Brenton
You're just used to your queen-sized bed! If you were in the Navy, this would be normal life for you. Dr. Linda, are those bunk beds?

Dr. Linda
Yes, they are. That does look like the sleeping quarters of the ship. Now I'm trying to guide the camera into this little room beyond that door.

Danielle
That looks like an old stove! Is that the kitchen?

Dr. Linda
It sure is! It was called the cooking galley of the ship.

Dr. Linda
Well, it's about time for us to leave our sunken ship full of undiscovered treasures and return to solid land. Are you ready?

Danielle, Trenton, and Brenton
NO!

Dr. Linda
We don't want to disturb this fragile ecosystem for too long. Let's look at the sea creatures on our way back up. Perhaps I'll put another adventure up for bidding on the Internet. Maybe I'll see you again someday soon! Until the next undersea discovery . . . .

Developing Reading Fluency • Gr. 5 © 2004 Creative Teaching Press

The Commercial

Characters: Pat   Arthur
                  Ellie   Sandy

Arthur

Hello to our viewers! We hope you're having a terrific day!

Pat

Don't go away! Stay right on that couch! We have a very special offer for you.

Ellie

That's right! It's available for today only!

Sandy

It's only for viewers of "Crazy Cartoon Capers"! That's you!

Arthur

Today, we are offering the Handy Dandy Cotton Candy Maker.

Pat

That's right! You can have fresh, warm, gooey cotton candy that melts in your mouth!

Ellie

What's the price you ask? Well, have we got a special offer for you today! You can buy this Handy Dandy Cotton Candy Maker at the low introductory price of only $12.99!

Sandy

That's right! She said only $12.99! What a deal!

Arthur

If you looked on the Internet or in your local stores, you'd find a similar machine for at least $50.00. That's right, I said $50.00!

Developing Reading Fluency • Gr. 5 © 2004 Creative Teaching Press

Reader's Theater

The Commercial

Pat

What's even more important is the quality of our product! Your complete satisfaction is guaranteed!

Ellie

In fact, if you're not completely satisfied that the Handy Dandy Cotton Candy Maker is the best product at the cheapest price on the market, then we'll refund your money plus give you an extra $5.00!

Sandy

You heard her right! If you don't LOVE the Handy Dandy Cotton Candy Maker, then we'll gladly take it back.

Arthur

You'd better hurry! We have a limited supply of only 1,000 at this special introductory price. When those are sold, we'll be raising the price to $19.99.

Pat

Don't let the other "Cartoon Caper" viewers beat you to this special deal. Run to your parents! Tell them about this incredible bargain!

Ellie

What? You don't think your parents will want to buy a machine that makes cotton candy? You've got to be kidding!

Sandy

Cotton candy is cheaper and easier to make than cookies! It's healthier than a bag of chips!

Arthur

Best of all, this Handy Dandy Cotton Candy Maker is kid-tested, parent-approved! It's safe for you to make the cotton candy all by yourself!

Pat

That's right! That means never having to bother your parents in the middle of their work to make you a tasty treat.

Developing Reading Fluency • Gr. 5 © 2004 Creative Teaching Press

The Commercial

Ellie

Imagine coming home from school to a yummy cotton candy treat you can make yourself!

Sandy

Oh, no! I've just gotten the word that we are down to our last 50 machines!

Arthur

Don't delay! Students just like you are buying this Handy Dandy Cotton Candy Maker right this minute.

Pat

Don't be left out! Everyone wants one!

Ellie

To take advantage of this introductory offer, all you have to do is call the number on your screen!

Sandy

Make sure you have your parent's permission. We don't want to sell the Handy Dandy Cotton Candy Maker to families that wouldn't appreciate the fine craftsmanship our machine has to offer.

Arthur

Hurry! Time is running out! Dial 1-800-555-5555 to get the Handy Dandy Cotton Candy Maker at the low, low price of only $12.99! We'll be waiting by the phones while you go back to watching your cartoons. Call us now! We're waiting for you!

Developing Reading Fluency • Gr. 5 © 2004 Creative Teaching Press

Kids in Business

Characters: Kimberly   Elizabeth
Bob   Narrator

Narrator
Kimberly, Elizabeth, and Bob need money! They are each trying to save for their college expenses when they grow up, while getting new clothes and fun toys right now. In order to have both, they've decided that they will have to start a business.

Bob
Kimberly, you and I are so good with animals. I think we'd make good dog walkers!

Elizabeth
I want to be in the business, too. I think we should offer to pick up people's newspapers when they're out of town.

Kimberly
That's a good idea, but people don't always go out of town so we wouldn't make very much money.

Bob
For safety reasons, Mom would only let us do it for the neighbors we know, so that makes even fewer people. I agree with Kimberly. It's a good idea, but we need a business idea that would generate more chances to earn money.

Elizabeth
Why don't we just ask Mom to start giving us an allowance so we won't have to open a business at all?

Bob
You know what Mom thinks, "The harder you work, the more you'll appreciate what you have."

Kimberly
I know what she means, but I'm only in fifth grade! All of my friends get an allowance. It's just not fair!

Developing Reading Fluency • Gr. 5 © 2004 Creative Teaching Press

Kids in Business

Bob

Whether or not we agree with Mom's decision doesn't matter. We don't get an allowance, so we need to figure out how to earn money. Starting our own business is a smart idea. Let's see what other ideas we can think of. Maybe if we made a list we could all vote on our top three ideas. With any luck, we'll all choose the same business!

Elizabeth

Great idea! Did you already write down dog walkers and newspaper collectors? I think you should add car washers to the list.

Narrator

They all walked over to the kitchen table. Bob took out a pad of paper and began his list.

Kimberly

You've got to be kidding! I'm not washing any cars! My nails will get dirty. You'd better come up with a better idea than that.

Narrator

Kimberly was never very fond of the idea of work.

Bob

I know! We could offer to mow the neighbors' lawns.

Elizabeth

Easy for you to say. I'd be lucky if I could push the lawn mower even one foot. Let's keep thinking. There must be something we could do that people would be willing to pay for.

Kimberly

Maybe we should think about something we could make and sell instead of trying to sell a service. Some people would rather get something for their money.

Elizabeth

Do you mean like a bake sale?

Developing Reading Fluency • Gr. 5 © 2004 Creative Teaching Press

Kids in Business

Bob

That would be fun, but a bake sale only earns money once. We need a business that can continue to sell our product. Besides, you know how much Mom worries about us eating foods made by strangers. I'm sure other parents feel the same way. Baking food probably should be out of the question.

Kimberly

I guess you're right. "Safety first!" Mom always says.

Narrator

By now they are running out of ideas. They are all sitting at the table, thinking about what they could do. Suddenly, Elizabeth jumps up and says . . .

Elizabeth

I've got it! I have the perfect business for us! Kimberly, what do you love to do in your spare time?

Kimberly

Draw. Why?

Elizabeth

Bob, what do you love to do when you get some free time?

Bob

You mean besides read? I love to build things.

Elizabeth

That's right, and what do I love to do? I love to make scrapbooks and design creative things, right? If you put all of our talents together, what do you get?

Narrator

Bob and Kimberly are totally confused. They are trying to figure out what Elizabeth's idea could possibly be. Eventually, Elizabeth can't wait any longer to share her brilliant business plan.

Elizabeth

We could make greeting cards and sell them to our neighbors, friends, family, and troop leaders! Isn't that a fabulous idea?

Developing Reading Fluency • Gr. 5 © 2004 Creative Teaching Press

Kids in Business

Narrator

Bob and Kimberly think about it for a minute. Then, Bob says . . .

Bob

How does my love of building things fit into a greeting card business?

Elizabeth

We need display stands, greeting card boxes, and a large box to keep them organized! You see, it's perfect for each of us.

Bob

It would give us a chance to have an ongoing money-making opportunity.

Kimberly

Forget the list. We need to make a business plan!

Narrator

Instead of making a list of possible business options, they listed the supplies they would need to get started.

Kimberly

Wait a minute! We don't have any money, right? All of these supplies will cost us money. We can't make the greeting cards without the supplies. How can we solve that problem?

Bob

In school, we learned about the stock market. My teacher, Ms. Colby, taught us that some companies get money by letting people invest in them.

Kimberly

Right! You offer an incentive, such as a portion of your profits, to people who are willing to loan you the money you need to start your business.

Narrator

Suddenly, it came to them all at the same time. They knew whom to invite to invest!

Elizabeth, Bob, and Kimberly   *(loudly)*
Mom?

Developing Reading Fluency • Gr. 5 © 2004 Creative Teaching Press

Intervention Activities

Every section in this book can be used throughout the year to teach, guide, practice, and reinforce reading with phrasing and fluency, which will improve students' reading comprehension. The following activities provide additional practice and instruction for those students who need more help with the strategies that will help them improve their reading fluency. Assess students' stage of fluency by referring to the chart on page 7.

Use the following activities with "robotic readers" to help them be successful. The activities in this section will help students focus on the following strategies: phrased reading, automaticity with high-frequency words and phrases, recognition of what fluency sounds like at the listening level, and active listening.

Each activity includes an objective, a materials list, and step-by-step instructions. The activities are best suited to individualized instruction or very small groups. The activities can be adapted for use with larger groups or a whole-class setting in some cases.

Phrasing Cards

Strategies: explicit phrasing; automaticity with common phrases; modeled reading; repeated reading

Objective: Each student will practice reading the phrases with increasing speed and accuracy.

Materials
- Phrasing Cards (pages 86–89)
- Reading Rate Progress Plotter (page 90)
- card stock
- scissors
- 2 binder rings
- timer

Directions

1. Photocopy both sets of cards on card stock. Laminate the cards for durability. The first set consists of two- to three-word phrases. The second set has mostly four-word phrases. Use Set 1 before Set 2. Your goal is to have students read four- to five-word phrases by the end of fifth grade.

2. Cut apart the cards, and hole-punch them. Put them on two different rings—Set 1 and Set 2—for fast flipping.

3. Photocopy the Reading Rate Progress Plotter for each student.

4. Get a timer to keep track of the time it takes a student to read the set of cards most appropriate for him or her.

5. Call the student over to a quiet space in the room for one-on-one instruction.

6. **Do NOT review the phrases or model before beginning this activity.** Your goal is to determine the student's baseline phrasing ability and then scaffold the learning.

7. When you are ready to start, begin the timer and flip the phrasing cards at a steady pace. Try to maintain this pace with all students each time. (For this reason, it is best not to use adult volunteers for this activity.)

8. As you flip, try your best to count the number of phrases the student actually reads word by word—not in phrases. This will help you discover the relationship between phrasing and speed for each student.

9. Record the student's reading rate and the approximate number of phrases read as phrases (not word by word).

10. Immediately **after** the student finishes, go through and model the reading of one phrase at a time. Have the student repeat after you. Repeat this step one more time.

11. Repeat the ten steps listed above every day for ten consecutive days. Move the student from Set 1 to Set 2 when he or she can read each phrase in under 4 seconds.

Phrasing Cards: Set 1
(2- to 3-word common phrases)

you and I	the people
he called me	one more time
not now	sit down
now and then	each of us
he has it	in the end
but not me	we were here
all day long	it's about time
which way	some people
what happened next	right now
put it there	going under
help me out	give it away
it never happened	in the beginning

Developing Reading Fluency • Gr. 5 © 2004 Creative Teaching Press

Phrasing Cards: Set 1
(2- to 3-word common phrases)

in each case	for these reasons
over time	just in time
and so on	have been able
in other words	for example
as a result	a couple of
as with many	may one day
in that place	it is likely
just too soon	could already see
he couldn't see	I think so
close the door	I miss you
on my side	a good thought
because of that	do it often

Intervention Activities

Phrasing Cards: Set 2
(4-word common phrases)

end of the day	are among the best
and in the end	as if he were
on the way back	once upon a time
all of a sudden	a new way of
on top of the	she could see that
he tried to think	at the next place
in the first place	just could not understand
the best way to	so in the end
as big as the	the very next day
in a long time	now is the time
a number of people	once in a while
what they will do	more than the other

Developing Reading Fluency • Gr. 5 © 2004 Creative Teaching Press

Phrasing Cards: Set 2

(4-word common phrases)

in so many ways	but on the way
a list of ways	what have you learned
so they could see	she thought about it
go through with it	about to get caught
get over the fact	a couple of times
to see how they	they could not decide
which do you think	compare the two ways
on the other hand	later on that day
the interesting thing is	the main reason why
in such a hurry	put part of it
in addition to that	once there was a
tried to find it	and then what happened

Developing Reading Fluency • Gr. 5 © 2004 Creative Teaching Press

Intervention Activities

Reading Rate Progress Plotter

Name				
Date	Reading Rate	Rubic Score	Number of Correct Phrases	Growth?

Name				
Date	Reading Rate	Rubic Score	Number of Correct Phrases	Growth?

Developing Reading Fluency • Gr. 5 © 2004 Creative Teaching Press

Roll a Phrase

Strategies: explicit phrasing; repeated reading; phrases in writing

Objective: Each student will dictate and/or write five sentences with the rolled phrases. The student will break up the sentences into phrased, meaningful chunks.

Materials
- Roll a Phrase dice (page 92)
- dry erase board or paper
- dry erase marker or pencils

Directions

1. Photocopy the dice on page 92. Cut out the dice, and laminate them for durability. Form the dice by taping the sides together.

2. Invite one or two students to work with you in a quiet area of the room.

3. Model the activity by rolling the dice. Say the phrases that are rolled in a clear phrased voice. Make up a sentence or sentences using the phrases. Model correct phrasing. Have students repeat your sentence.

4. Invite one student to roll the dice. That student will then say the rolled phrases. If the student does not use correct phrasing, model and have the student repeat. Next, have the student say a sentence with the phrases in it. Repeat the student's sentence exactly the way he or she said it (with or without phrasing). Your goal is to train the student's ear to hear the phrased chunks within the spoken sentences.

5. Continue a few times until it appears the student can hear and speak in phrases.

6. Give the student a piece of paper or a dry erase board. Have him or her roll the dice again. Then, have the student write down a sentence in phrased chunks using the rolled phrases.

7. Read aloud the student's sentence.

Intervention Activities

Roll a Phrase

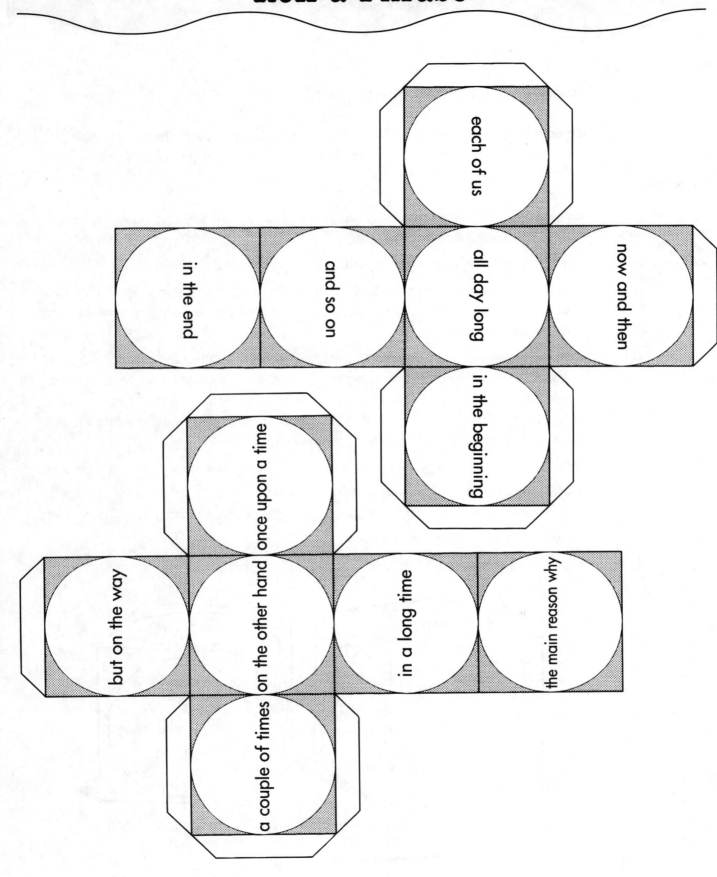

each of us

in the end

and so on

all day long

now and then

in the beginning

once upon a time

but on the way

on the other hand

in a long time

the main reason why

a couple of times

Strategies: explicit phrasing; repeated reading; choral reading; language experience

Objective: Each student will be able to reconstruct his or her own dictated sentences, which have been cut into phrases by the teacher. The student will then be able to read his or her own sentences with phrasing and fluency.

Materials
- black marker
- strips of paper
- scissors

Directions

1. Invite the student to tell you something fun he or she did over the weekend or is planning to do soon. Use a black marker to record on paper strips exactly what the student says. Limit his or her comments to a maximum of four sentences.

2. Arrange the strips so the student can read them.

3. Model how to read the sentences using phrasing, intonation, and fluency. (You may slightly exaggerate a slower pace.)

4. Have the student read and try to mimic the same phrasing, intonation, and fluency that you modeled.

5. Reread the phrases, but stop at each phrase and cut the strip. You will now have a set of phrases.

6. Mix up the phrases.

7. Tell the student to reconstruct the sentences in proper sequence by moving the strips around. Ask the student to leave gaps between the strips so he or she can visualize the places to break when reading and train his or her eyes to see chunks of words.

8. Every time the student adds another phrase to a sentence, have him or her reread. This will provide the repeated reading in phrased chunks necessary for transfer.

9. Once the student has put together an entire sentence, he or she should have already read and reread it many times. Now the student should be able to reread the phrases with the expected phrasing, intonation, and fluency. Have the student repeat step 8 with the strips for the remaining sentences.

My mother and I

went to the aquarium

to see the dolphins.

Intervention Activities

Strategies: modeled phrased reading; repeated reading

Objective: Each student will be able to listen for and hear the phrased units in text and then repeat them with the same phrasing, intonation, and fluency.

Materials
- 2 tape recorders
- cassette tapes
- headset

Directions

1. In advance, have a clear, fluent adult reader read one paragraph from a classroom book and record it three times as follows:
- Read the paragraph clearly and fluently
- Read the paragraph one phrase at a time—stopping long enough for the student to repeat it the exact way
- Reread the paragraph clearly and fluently.

2. Send the student to a quiet area of the room with a copy of the paragraph. Have him or her listen to the first reading. Then, have the student listen to the second reading and repeat each phrase after the speaker. Have the student listen to the third reading. Finally, have the student read aloud the paragraph on his or her own.

3. When the student understands what to do, turn on both tape recorders. Make sure that the student is following along in the book. Play the prerecorded tape on the first player. Make sure that the second player is recording.

4. Play back the tape of the student reading alone. Discuss observations related to phrasing, intonation, speed, and overall fluency.

Strategies: explicit phrasing instruction; peer tutoring

Objective: Each student will be able to create a mini-book for a kindergarten or first-grade student, modeling for the younger student how to read the chunked phrases in a mini-book.

Materials
- Jump, Frog, Jump! reproducible (page 96)
- plain paper
- scissors
- glue
- crayons or markers

Directions

1. Ask a kindergarten or first-grade teacher to identify a student who can read words in isolation, but who does not read with any phrasing or fluency.

2. Tell your fifth grader that he or she will have a chance to be a teacher. Explain that the younger student is still learning the basics of reading.

3. Give the student plain paper, scissors, glue, and crayons or markers. Have the student use the Jump, Frog, Jump! reproducible to create a mini-book about a frog. Have him or her cut out each phrase and glue it to the appropriate page as indicated on the chart. Then, have the student draw an illustration to accompany each phrase.

4. Have the student follow the Fantastic Five Format (see page 8) and use the mini-book to teach the young buddy how to read with phrasing and fluency.

Jump, Frog, Jump!

Page		
Cover	Jump, Frog, Jump!	
1	Once upon a time	
2	there was a frog.	
3	He jumped	on a lilypad.
4	He jumped	on a log.
5	He jumped	on a flower.
6	He jumped	on a bee.
7	He jumped	on a ladybug.
8	He jumped	on me!

Developing Reading Fluency • Gr. 5 © 2004 Creative Teaching Press